FREEDOM AND AUTHORITY
IN EDUCATION

by the same author

*

EDUCATION IN AN INDUSTRIAL SOCIETY
EDUCATION AND VALUES

Geoffrey Herman

G. H. BANTOCK, 1914 -

FREEDOM AND AUTHORITY
IN EDUCATION ;

A Criticism of Modern Cultural
and Educational Assumptions ·

The Rev. Dr. Opimian: *If all the nonsense which, in the last quarter of a century, has been talked on all other subjects were thrown into one scale, and all that has been talked on the subject of education alone were thrown into the other, I think the latter would preponderate.*
—THOMAS LOVE PEACOCK: *Gryll Grange*

FABER & FABER LIMITED
24 Russell Square
London

First published in mcmlii
by Faber and Faber Limited
24 Russell Square London WC1
Second edition mcmlxv 1965
Printed in Great Britain by
Latimer Trend & Co Ltd Whitstable

FOR JEAN

PREFACE

One, at least, of the functions of this book is to stimulate controversy on the most pressing educational problem of our day, the purposes and limitations of the so-called 'progressive' movement. This movement has two facets—one which encourages individual 'self-expression', the other which urges 'group' activities. It is my thesis that both aspects of the movement are based on an inadequate comprehension of the human situation; and I seek to invoke a fuller understanding of what is implied by the claims of 'freedom' and 'authority' in the modern world, in terms of which day to day educational practices will take on a juster significance. For only out of a profound realization of what is involved in the nature of life will come an adequate educational philosophy. And I wish to urge that attention to these problems of educational 'philosophy' is intensely practical—is, indeed, demanded by the too naïve acceptance (and, in some cases, rejection) of the 'progressive' movement.

A considerable part of this book has been printed as separate articles in *Scrutiny*, *The Cambridge Journal*, *The Times Educational Supplement* and the A.T.C.D.E. *Bulletin*. Acknowledgements and thanks are due to the editors of these journals for kind permission to reprint. All the articles have, however, been revised —in some cases extensively—and in most cases new matter added. Acknowledgements and thanks are also due to Mrs. Frieda Lawrence and to Messrs. William Heinemann Ltd. for generous permission to quote extracts from the work of D. H. Lawrence.

PREFACE

I am most grateful to Mr. Boris Ford for having replied to Chapter Three, as it originally appeared in *Scrutiny* and for thus having stimulated that interchange of views and criticism of assumptions which is so urgent a need in current educational thinking. Mr. Ford's essay represented the best sort of collaboration that one can seek at this juncture. Mr. P. A. W. Collins kindly read the essay on Newman, and made several suggestions for which I was most grateful. Finally, most thanks are due to my wife for having typed the manuscript, prepared the index and, above all, for having discussed the book with me and led me to undertake many clarifications.

G. H. BANTOCK

University College, Leicester
February 1952

INTRODUCTION
TO THE SECOND EDITION

When this book first appeared in 1952 it achieved a minor *succès de scandale*. It was judged scandalous by some sections of educational opinion because it questioned what, so far as the conscious articulation of educational theory was concerned, had, for a time, been the accepted orthodoxy (I put it this way because progressivism affected educationists more than it did schools—the grammar schools, for instance, were largely, though not completely, untouched; only the infant schools underwent a major revolution). Futhermore, it said some sharp things about current educational theorising and the poor quality of much of the writing in the field, things which, whilst they delighted the hearts of some, were obviously much too tough-minded for many in a sphere where the tender-minded had held sway for so long. The result was that the book attracted partisanship rather than serious evaluation and criticism; and there were times when it needed to be defended from its friends as well as from its enemies. It was probably a mistake to make it quite so polemical in tone, because it was, in general, taken to be exclusively an attack on progressivism rather than an examination of that movement. Obviously, there was much in progressivism which was found wanting—an inadequate metaphysic and psychology of man as well as an unconvincing ethic; but, to say that I was spurred on by a 'passionate dislike' of the progressive movement, as did the reviewer in the then *Manchester Guardian*,

I

was something less than just. Indeed, progressive notions in education had played a considerable part in my own mental development; and it may surprise readers to learn that I consider W. B. Curry's little book on *The School*—Curry was then the headmaster of Dartington Hall—to have had a quite crucial effect on the growth of my intellectual self-dependence; I read it soon after I left school. For a time, I counted myself an ardent progressive and looked back on my own schooldays with a certain self-pitying regret. Actual experience and the passing of the years convinced me that neither life nor education were as simple as Mr. Curry's enunciation of his principles made them out to be. Nevertheless, when I stated some of the benefits which child-centred notions had conferred on our thinking about education [pp. 60–62], welcomed the new movement in art teaching [p. 75], approved 'directed play' methods* [p. 65] and made a number of other comments intended to welcome the stimulus that 'progressive' notions had afforded us, I meant to be taken seriously. And the critic who urged my support for his own dislike of Caldwell Cook's *The Play Way* and who asserted that, surely, I would disapprove of such idle and irrelevant methods in the teaching of English would, alas, have been disappointed. Caldwell Cook's *Play Way*, for all its turgidity of style and occasional embarrassment of terminology, was a book which I invariably recommended to my students who were training as teachers of English. Worse, I used to cart them, year after year, to witness the teaching, at the Perse School, Cambridge, of one of Cook's last pupils, who had revitalised and rejuvenated the work of his former master, the late Douglas Brown. There, Douglas, a supremely great teacher and a brilliant mind, demonstrated what a liberal understanding of English studies could achieve with generations of school boys; and it was undeniably 'play way', interpreted with intelligence and rigour. His early

* Undirected play, vital though it is for the development of children, seems to me to have little place in the school except for deprived children; for play in school is necessarily play under supervision—and, therefore, must inevitably lack the spontaneity and unselfconsciousness which is an important part of true play. Under the heading of 'directed' play I would certainly include creative play involving mime, movement, dance, etc.

death has robbed English education of a seminal mind and the university which had appointed him Professor of English of a brilliant scholar—and his friends of a warm and generous personality.

Progressivism, then, had made the child more important; and it had added some useful techniques to our repertoire in teaching. My feeling that, at the time, these benefits were not what needed stressing, was quite genuine. For I had seen too much of the confusion and uncertainty that the application of progressive principles had generated in the minds of students, both where teaching and their own learning were concerned, to remain satisfied with progressivism as I saw it applied in training college and department of education. Frequently, of course, there was a misunderstanding of theory—progressivism was a complicated and difficult theory (or set of theories) to understand and to put into practice. But, often, such confusion sprang from shortcomings in the theories themselves. Progressivism's view of human nature was too naive, its purposes too little concentrated on what I thought—and still think—to be the main aim of the school—to promote certain specific types of learning. Teaching, after all, involved a triadic relationship; subject matter was as important as the child. Also, progressivism strove to be too all-embracing in its concern for what it vaguely termed the 'whole child'. Indeed, it comprised a social ethic as well as a theory of learning, and it depended on which aspect of the theory one happened to favour as to whether that ethic appeared in its liberal (self-expressive) or collectivist (group co-operative) guise. Both, indeed, seemed to me inadequate as formulated by the main progressive thinkers; and both, in their different ways, contained implicit threats to our cherished freedom.* For, paradoxically enough in view of the comments

* I was charged, at the time, with concentrating my attack on the lesser progressive thinkers; I should, it was implied, have discussed more the work of the giants. There is some truth in this accusation; my reason for not dealing more thoroughly with writers of the stature of Rousseau and Dewey was two-fold. I had in mind, then, the writing of a history of progressive education (which I may still accomplish) and, obviously, these two would play an important part in that; secondly, I wanted to tackle what was

it attracted, my book seems to me, on a re-reading, to be at least as much about freedom as it is about authority; it considers the latter, indeed, only in so far as it is relevant to the former. The book is concerned to put forward a theory of freedom in education which is analogous to one that Mr. Maurice Cranston in a little book published not long after my own appeared, called a theory of rational freedom; though there was also an indication that, on occasions, at least where children are concerned, what was needed was a theory of compulsory rational freedom. According to these theories, freedom was not simply something that stood opposed to various possible constraints—'freedom from', in fact. It was 'something realised', to be worked for, either through internal restraints (rational freedom) or through external ones (compulsory rational freedom); it involved 'freedom to', that is to say. Where children are concerned, it is not unjustifiable to suggest that their coming to freedom should involve a development from compulsory rational freedom to rational freedom as the discipline of learning needs to be less externally imposed and becomes more a matter of internal self-direction. The crucial thing, however, is that these are theories of rational freedom, which invoke—even if they do not logically depend on—a very different metaphysic of man from that implicit in progressivism. For the latter remains strongly influenced by Rousseauesque optimism, so that the belief in the 'natural goodness' of man seems to involve largely the lifting of restraints. But my study of both Rousseau and Dewey and my observation of actual progressive practice convinced me that there was a degree of fraud involved here; always some element of authority was smuggled in. Rousseau, for instance, was not consistent in his theory of 'negative' education; and, indeed, his whole mode of education in *Emile* can appear to involve the most drastic interference with the 'free' self-development of the individual, as being said at the moment. So I published my views on Rousseau and Dewey in article form rather than as part of a book. However, in view of the fact that my attempt to write the history of progressive education has been held up, I have published both now in book form—that on Rousseau in *Education and Values* and that on Dewey in *Education in an Industrial Society*.

4

when he utters the ultimate in educational tyranny: 'He should only do what he wants to do; *but he should only want to do what you want him to do.*' [My italics]. Rousseau's attempt to provide a total environment for his pupil seems to me to deprive him even of the choice implicit in rebellion. This was the logical consequence of attempting to make man a moral creature without involving him in the personal conflicts out of which morality could grow. Those who put forward theories of rational freedom see man as, 'naturally', the prey to conflicting forces. It is the latter metaphysic which lies behind my own views and those of my witnesses, including (usually) D. H. Lawrence.

All formulations, whether of criticism or of positive principles, depend on certain key concepts which the writer normally takes for granted. In this book, one of these is the notion of 'concreteness'; and one of the more serious commentators on it, Miss H. M. Adams of the University of Edinburgh, took me to task for accusing my opponents of 'making their case through "emotive" terms' whilst being 'open to the charge of making [my] own case through the invocation of terms as emotionally charged and equally unanalysed'; and she mentions 'concrete', 'submission' and 'utilitarian'. I don't altogether see the difficulty with the two latter; but 'concrete' does, perhaps, require some elucidation. It is, it must be admitted, a relative term; and my use of it owes something to the criticism of Dr. F. R. Leavis. Men live by abstracting, through the various symbolic modes they have developed, such aspects of the totality presented to them by the external world as meet their requirements; these abstractions add up to the various structures of knowledge and understanding (cognitive and emotional) which constitute man's conscious life. But some of these structures of abstractions exist on a higher level of generality than others. It is of the nature of science, for instance, to subsume particular observations under general laws. Forms of artistic observation, usually, tend to work the other way; though still abstractions from the totality of the presented world, what artists produce tends to be rooted in a particular scene, a particular situation; where they achieve what used to be called 'universality', they do it through a close scrutiny of a particular happening or setting. It is to this greater particularity of effect that I have applied the term 'concrete'. Social scientists try to produce generalisations relevant to the crime of murder; Shakespeare, in *Macbeth*, gives us a specific murderer, prey to a particular temptation, revealing through the way he speaks—the rhythms his voice unconsciously adopts—and the things he says, the tensions implicit in his ambitions, his fears, his desire to act the man as his wife has cast the rôle, and his apprehensions of the intangible sanctions that, in his times, awaited the imprudent sinner. Because we are moved emotionally as well as intellectually by what we read in the play, our awareness of human behaviour is both widened and deepened; what has been provoked is a mode of concrete thinking about human behaviour *less* abstract, it seems to me, than that provoked by the social scientist, and also one permitting qualitative considerations peculiarly helpful in considering education with its built-in moral concern. It is this type of approach to human problems, as a supplement to, rather than as a replacement of, what the social scientist can provide, which lies behind my use of the word 'concrete'—one still abstract, in some degree, but involving a wider range of human modes of apprehension than is usually relied upon by the scientist; it leads, perhaps, to empathy as well as to purely abstract 'understanding', as one understands, say, the statistics relating to capital punishment. As Eliot said of understanding a culture: 'either it is abstract—and the essence escapes—or it is *lived*'. The artist can, in some respects, take us nearer to what it is to live a culture than can the social investigator. This is why the insights of literary artists are more informative about some of the crucial problems in education than are those, in general, of the educational researchers, and why I persist in finding T. S. Eliot and D. H. Lawrence, as I have stated elsewhere,* the two who have had the most cogent things to say about education in our times.

I feel that it is only reasonable that I should provide this extended analysis of what is, indeed, a key notion in my book

* cf. *Education and Values.*

in view of my own strictures on current looseness of expression. My concern here was perhaps semantic rather than one fully informed by the philosophic habit of linguistic analysis. This may partly be because I have always regarded analysis only as a propaedeutic; I wanted to go on to make those prescriptions which modern philosophers, at least in 1952, shrank from. (There are signs that my point of view on this has perhaps come to be more widely accepted by philosophers in the intervening fourteen years.) Nevertheless, I was concerned at what Professor Richard Peters has recently called the 'mush' of theorising where education was concerned. The reasons for the comparative immaturity of educational thinking in any of the relevant fields—particularly in the philosophic one—are probably connected with the particular way in which education departments have evolved in universities. Their development has been bound up, not with specific academic disciplines relevant to the study of education, but with the practical necessities of training teachers. This has meant that the majority of the appointed staff have been subject specialists who have taken up the study of 'education' as an afterthought and often without any specific training in the relevant fields. This may account for the fact that what has traditionally passed for the philosophy of education has been a number of gentlemanly reflections on education by people who have had some actual experience of teaching but very little professionalised discipline in what to-day, in this country, constitutes philosophy. I was myself sufficiently aware of some of the implications of the 'recent revolution' (dating from the early years of the century) to want to provide something more stringent; but sufficiently out of sympathy with the moral neutrality which modern ethical theory implied to want to provide something more directly evaluative (Mr. Cranston, for instance, suggests that 'rational' theories of freedom may constitute value judgements). Thus, I insulted the gentlemanly purveyors of ripe wisdom in education, without altogether pleasing the philosophers. The latter, though in a number of cases agreeing with what one termed 'my programme'—by which he intended my defence of academic values—were uneasy at the mixture of analysis and evaluation, as I have hinted above, and did not altogether appreciate an approach which stemmed from literary 'thought' rather than from a more orthodox philosophical standpoint.

I can only urge that, however inadequate my practice, I helped to open a fruitful vein. For one thing, I brought the comparatively recent ('comparatively', because there was what is recognisably progressive teaching in the eighteenth century) manifestation of progressive thinking into relation to writers who had evolved out of a tradition of effort and creation which stretched back through the centuries. Especially fascinating in this respect was D. H. Lawrence, superficially appearing so progressive, in reality so deeply aware of the need for roots and of the pain of effort that went into true creativity. The literary tradition is one which is rooted in an awareness of social and individual complexities such as any educationist needs to be aware of. My use of it was a means of stressing the need for continuity as against a theory which had been deeply affected by Rousseau's neurotic distaste for the traditions of his society —and yet it stemmed from men who had themselves bequeathed genuinely new insights to their respective ages, who existed as living manifestations of Eliot's dictum that 'tradition cannot mean standing still'. Our society, in the view of education that it encourages, is obsessed with the image of change which it believes itself to foster. What is forgotten is that changes are specific and that, whereas many such changes have, indeed, taken place, in many of the deepest human problems change is so slow as to be almost non-existent; so that, for instance, when Freud thought he had discovered something fundamental about a stage of human development, he gave it a name drawn from Greek mythology. Life must be lived forwards—but, paradoxically, it can only be so lived in terms of the experience gleaned from the past. Continuity is not a device for strengthening the inert hand of the dead; it is an essential element in the successful evolution of the new. Progressivism, by being too little conscious of history, denies itself the fruition it so ardently desires.

I cannot think that, since the book first appeared, the cultural

8

situation which evoked my stress on standards, a comparative indifference to which was one of the manifestations which provoked the book, has improved. In this sense, at least, the book is as relevant to-day as when it was first written. What, indeed, has happened in the intervening fourteen years has been the gradual decline of interest in individual self-expression and a comparatively strong concern for the collectivity. Dewey and Mannheim, rather than Rousseau, lie behind the current concern for social unity; the instruments of this concern are the organisational devices of the comprehensive school and the unstreamed class—though Mannheim wouldn't altogether fit here, because he was still far too interested in the importance of the *élite*. In the latter years of the nineteenth century the sensitive were made to feel guilty if they had too much money—not, by any means, a wholly unjust process of sensitisation to the economic needs of others. During the last fifteen years, however, the process has been extended, by some, to those who happen to possess more brains (unless they are likely to aid the drive for productivity)—a much more doubtful procedure. The story of Mishmar Haemek no longer seems quite so remote from English practice as once it did. Drastic changes in the organisation of secondary education are made not so much because of the gross inefficiency of the present system—the vexed problem of selection could have been mitigated by a blurring of edges within the tripartite system—but, in part at least, because brains don't apparently come forward in sufficient numbers from the right section of the community and our social consciences are offended by the spectacle of what appears privilege for the more intellectually able. The *avant-garde* in education is no longer so bothered by the uncreative environment and its stultification of individual creativity (for, however inadequate a view of creation it fostered, progressivism did, at least, keep the notion before our consciousnesses); instead, it urges the necessities of social consensus and looks to the schools to heal the rifts caused by class divisions. The fact that the divisions occur increasingly in terms of ability, rather than birth, doesn't assuage the egalitarians.

The comprehensive school, indeed, with its concern for the common curriculum (for the first two or three years, at least) is the apostle of the common culture, in the exposition of which similar verbal prevarications and jugglings to those which marked Mannheim's concern for popularisation appear—and in much the same cause: that all should share the same experiences, but at different levels. I can't help feeling, then, that what I have to say about the 'essentials' of, and the 'really human elements' in, knowledge, in my criticism of Mannheim, is still relevant, more specifically so, indeed, where practices in schools are concerned, than when it first appeared. A comprehensive school headmaster, not long ago, urged the importance of manner of presentation rather than differentiation of content in teaching the various strata in his school; it was as if the *same* content could, perhaps, be presented in different ways according to level of ability.

Critical of progressivism though I am, I can't help feeling that it represented, in its more characteristic self-expressive guise, something a good deal more interesting, educationally speaking, than does the present concern for educational organisation. At least it took us nearer the classroom and made us think a good deal about the individual child. When I re-read my book, I find that there is very little that I would, fourteen years later, want to retract, though I might want to express some of it a little less brashly. I would merely want to sharpen those sections where I have pointed to the benefits that progressivism has bestowed on our thinking about education—particularly in our concern for the education of less able children.[1] If I have a general criticism to offer, it is that I saw educational problems too much from the point of view of that high culture in terms of which my own education had been carried out. I have, since, made some amends for this in my more recently published *Education in an Industrial Society*, where I attempt to see the problem of the bulk of our school population from the radically different angle which I think is needed.

[1] Extensive alteration, in any case, would have been impossible because the book is being re-published by photographic means.

Even here, what is wanted is a disciplined attention; and, though I think that, for instance, Dewey's conception of progressivism sprang out of an attempt to find incentives for leaning on the part of the dispossessed, I find his educational programme too involved with a sort of social thinking which has, I think, little basis in social reality. Like most progressives, he, too, wavers between permissiveness and direction, except that his direction exists on behalf of the collectivity rather than in terms of that cultural liberation that I, myself, want to encourage.

In the last resort, it seems to me, educators must accept their responsibilities; even decisions to stand aside, to free children *from* restraints, are necessarily their decisions. But they must learn to temper responsibility with imagination. In so far as progressivism has helped to foster that imagination—and it has played a part in my own case—it has earned its place in our educational thinking; but that is no reason why it should not itself be subject to a rigorous scrutiny—and this is what I tried to provide.

CONTENTS

CHAPTER ONE

SCIENTIA SCIENTIARUM:
THE CURRENT CONFUSION

'The belief that men may continue to educate without concerning themselves with the subtle problems of philosophy means a failure to understand the precise nature of education.'
—GENTILE

Confusion about the ends and aims of education is no new thing; Aristotle noted it in the society of his time. Even ages of reasonable stability and homogeneous culture have admitted heterodox ideas. A time of accelerated social change, such as we are now enduring, when the very notion of orthodoxy has suffered an eclipse, can be expected to produce a variety of educational prescriptions. At the moment even those most ardently intent on swimming with the stream are a little puzzled into which of the confluence of courses they can most safely plunge. The old world has its supporters. The Greek ideal of the harmonious balance of personality is still invoked; Christian education has its apologists, and the 'common core', designed to introduce a whole population to its cultural inheritance, its advocates, albeit, often in equivocal terms. The public schools maintain their traditional ways, with some concessions to the zeitgeist; and even the classics have their last ditch defenders. But in a society that manifests itself in 'becoming' rather than 'being', the emphasis naturally tends to be on the new, the progressive, the necessity of meeting what is regarded as the novel situation in a rapidly evolving community. A network of lines of thought cross and merge here. There is a

13

basis of Benthamite scepticism, clearing the ground of dogma
and questioning the bases of authority; there is the Rousseauesque notion of the natural goodness of man to encourage the
fine 'spontaneous' rapture; there is—particularly potent—the
political doctrine of liberal egalitarianism, evoking the peren-
nial controversy between the claims of individual self-development and the democratic way of life; there is the scientific approach, with its concern for the quantitative and its technique
of the experiment (practically any piece of fatheadedness in
education can be excused on the grounds of experimentation);
there is the Comtist Positivistic Synthesis, manifesting itself, perhaps, as 'integration' or 'totality'; and there are no doubt others.
Any popular exposition of educational 'principles' may well
draw its assumptions from several of these infant traditions;
even as they stand, they merge; Comte, for instance, was greatly
influenced by scientific method.

In the balance of forces between the old and the new, then,
the progressives have it. In general the progressive movement
can be said to be humanistic and evolutionary rather than
apocalyptic and eschatological; it displays that contempt for
forms which De Tocqueville noted as the characteristic of
democratic philosophy. It is pragmatic rather than concerned
with ultimate aims, materialistic rather than idealistic. Hence
its neglect of ends, its emphasis on method and technique; for
technique involves process. It displays a scepticism before the
external world, and its reconstructions, such as they are, are
synthetical and rationalistic rather than derived from received
opinions and traditional modes. Its view of the individual is
atomistic rather than molecular; its group technique involves
an arbitrary imposition of coherence in face of the problem to
be ventilated rather than an organic effort by those with a
similar background of assumption. Hence it stands outside its
world and asks 'What is true?'—true, that is to say, to a particularly impoverished type of experience which the uniformity
of egalitarian life seems to foster; it does not accept and seek to
understand. It is thus ultimately an education of pride and
rejection rather than one of acceptance and humility. It in-

volves the decay of the intellect, the decline of the will and the triumph of impulse. For all its boast of vitality and its parade of joy, it lacks roots; and what lacks roots has a habit of bearing a stunted growth and withering.

Yet all revolutions, of course, are the products of a need. The coming to power of new classes has demanded a recognition of their plight and of their cultural disinheritance; or at least, of their disinheritance from that particular type of self-conscious culture which, in the past, has been the prerogative of the richer, upper and 'educated' classes. The sort of situation that George Bourne describes in *Change in the Village* could hardly go unrecognized in the changed political situation. Speaking of a young coal-carter, Bourne indicts his 'education':

'But it goes almost without saying that the man's "education" did very little to enrich his mind. The ideas and accomplishments he picked up at the elementary school between his fourth and fourteenth years were of course insufficient for the needs of a grown man, and it would be unfair to criticize his schooling from that standpoint. Its defect was that it failed to initiate him into the inner significance of information in general, and failed wholly to start him on the path of learning. It was sterile of results. It opened to him no view, no vista; set up in his brain no stir of activity such as could continue after he had left school; and this for the reason that those simple items of knowledge which it conveyed to him were too scrappy and too few to begin running together into any understanding of the larger aspects of life. A few rules of arithmetic, a little of the geography of the British Isles . . .; no inkling of the infinities of time and space, or of the riches of human thought; but merely a few "pieces" of poetry, and a few haphazard and detached observations (called "Nature Study" nowadays) about familiar things—"the cat", "the cow" . . . "the rainbow", and so forth—this was the jumble of stuff offered to the child's mind—a jumble to which it would puzzle a philosopher to give coherence. And what could a child get from it to kindle his enthusiasm for that civilized learning in which, none the less, it all may have its place?

When the boy left school his "education" had but barely begun.'

This indictment, it must be remembered, was not written by an educationalist with an axe to grind but by a profoundly humane person who saw how little the self-conscious elementary education had done to replace the profounder sanctions of the older agricultural and rural order.

But to admit the need is not to accept, wholesale, the outcome. Some good has resulted as we shall see;[1] and the attempt to bring education into relationship with life would evoke enthusiastic response were it not that what constitutes 'life' is often interpreted in too meagre a spirit. The time has arrived, it seems to me, to go closer to the fire and see what we are saying. After all, the profoundest philosophies of life are weakened in so far as they are diffused; they take their validity from the pressure of the originally conceiving mind, and they preserve that validity only in so far as the minds that grasp them maintain that pressure and thus keep intact the structure. When, however, notions that are not very profound to begin with are bandied about from mouth to mouth, become the common playthings of every mind which regards itself competent to judge— and such minds are numerous in our society—they rapidly lose what force they originally had. Such a situation seems to me to have arisen in current talk—it hardly merits the term 'theory' —about education. The tiresome iteration of current clichés, the vapidity of so much of the writing, the inexactness of the terminology used, the unawareness of implication or assumption shows that the time has come to call for a serious and sustained critical and philosophical effort. So much discussion on education has become a sort of 'phatic communion'; it recalls Dr. I. A. Richards's indictment of contemporary evaluative criticism:

'It is either suasion, which is politics, or it is social communion. As social communion (in a lecture, for example) it is a method of preparing the scene and conducting the occasion, of maintaining the civilizing convention that things are well,

---

[1] Cf. Chapter Three.

of inducing a reassured, easy and decorously receptive mood. It is a stream of gestures or ceremonies, a spirit-calming and mildly stimulating ritual.'[1]

A good example of the sort of thing I have in mind comes to hand during the week in which I write; it is taken from a recent presidential address to the Conference of Educational Associations: the passage chosen was picked out for particular commendation by *The Times Educational Supplement:*

'. . . in daily practice our freedom does largely depend upon how we behave to each other, and in that sense it becomes mainly a question of friendly and considerate relationship between all who constitute that varied cast engaged in the drama we call education . . . where there is a happy friendly spirit there, I submit, and there only freedom reigns.'

There is no sign, in the rest of the speech, of any understanding of what is implied by this 'friendly spirit', or by the group 'strategy' that the speaker's remarks are intended to foster. Place against this quotation the remarks of D. H. Lawrence in *Psychoanalysis and the Unconscious* and what I am getting at will perhaps become plainer:

'The amazingly difficult and vital business of human relationship has been almost laughably under-estimated in our epoch. All this nonsense about love and unselfishness more crude and repugnant than savage fetish-worship. Love is a thing to be *learned*, through centuries of patient effort. It is a difficult, complex maintenance of individual integrity throughout the incalculable processes of inter-human polarity.'

The juxtaposition of the two certainly displays, with a sharper focus, the insipidity of the former. Moreover remarks equally trite, equally lacking in personal pressure (such as that which the Lawrence displays, for instance) could be chosen from any educational journal any week. (Many of these journals themselves are over-ripe for critical comment, it could be said in passing.) Obviously one can hardly expect material of Law-

---

[1] *Practical Criticism*

rence's standard to crop up every week; what is disconcerting is the almost complete absence of any astringent thinking such as a learned profession might reasonably be expected to provide.

To ask for strenuousness of definition, of course, is to invite unpopularity in many circles. Discrimination of this kind is an act of the intellect—and the intellect, at the moment, is under something of a cloud. Moreover, those generous helpings of large abstractions—'freedom', 'wholeness', 'fruitful co-operation', 'integration', 'life', 'equal opportunity', 'citizenship'—induce a somnolent cosiness that it seems almost a pity to blow upon with a sharp wind of intellectual analysis. Yet if to define is to circumscribe and to limit, it is at the same time to sustain and to strengthen. Newman, in *A Grammar of Assent*, noted that it was a 'common mistake (to) suppose that there is a contrariety and antagonism between a dogmatic creed and vital religion'. Religion, he noted, is of the imagination, theology a construction of the mind. 'Theology may stand as a substantive science, though it be without the life of religion; but religion cannot maintain its ground at all without theology. Sentiment, whether imaginative or emotional, falls back upon the intellect for its stay, when sense cannot be called into exercise; and it is in this way that devotion falls back upon dogma.'

There seems to be a profound truth here, whose validity goes beyond the boundaries of religion and theology. Religion as 'sentiment', which came in for much of Newman's criticism, is, as he showed, inadequate; and the present indifference, after only three centuries of Protestantism, gives force to Newman's contention. Once the mind had given it a 'real assent', religion depended, as Newman saw, for its strength and permanence on the capacity of the mind to make those valid distinctions and definitions which are the province of theology. At the present moment, much writing on education seems to me to involve little more than expressions of sentiment, to be little more, in fact, than a series of vague gestures towards a formulation, gestures which rely for such impact as they make on the largely emotive significance of the words used. Education is thought to be a good thing, not because its advocates see in it an introduction to an immense labour of clarification about the external world, and one's relations to it, but because it has become the vehicle of a vague infusion of sentiment about something that can be best summed up in the cliché 'social living'. Education is in danger of losing all content beyond the range of a very limited series of social obligations; to place these obligations within their context, to circumscribe their incidence, ought to be seen as a vast effort of freeing rather than as restriction.

When, then, a serious and sustained critical and philosophic effort is suggested, what is being indicated is the sort of undertaking that Arnold desiderated: 'the endeavour, in all branches of knowledge, theology, philosophy, history, art, science, to see the object as in itself it really is.' To-day, it seems to me, our educationalists suffer from the same disease that afflicted the poets of the first half of the nineteenth century; they do not know enough. They suffer from that restriction of view that is one of the misfortunes of democracy, where 'every one shuts himself up in his own breast, and affects from that point to judge the world'. They accept no 'authority' beyond themselves. Hence, as in the early nineteenth century, that distaste for philosophy which De Tocqueville noted; that, combined with the English dislike of logic which the late Susan Stebbing remarked upon, their lazy-mindedness, their love of 'muddling through', does much to explain the prevalent laxity. What needs to be insisted on, in response to this apathy, is what Arnold insisted on: that such a critical effort would prove to be immensely creative—would, in fact, provide sustenance for that very 'creativity' that is so frequently invoked by modern educationalists, and which they so frequently regard, mistakenly, as the prerogative of the emotions only.

What sorts of things should be the objects of this critical study? To begin with, there might well be a probing and prodding of words; the halt, lame and footsore, those worn out with usage and ripe for retirement might well be put to hospital and there either nursed back to life or provided with decent burial. I suggest for clinical treatment: 'creativity', 'spontaneity', 'interest', 'development', 'social co-operation', 'integration', 'activity', 'joy of discovery', 'experience', 'living', 'expression', 'need', 'natural', 'freedom,' 'wholeness', 'growth', 'imagination'; readers can probably suggest many others. I need hardly stress this importance of language and terminology; as Ezra Pound said of words:

'When their very medium, the very essence of their work, the application of word to thing . . . becomes slushy and inexact, or excessive and bloated, the whole machinery of social and individual thought and order goes to pot.'

Nor, bearing in mind once more what De Tocqueville has to say, need one be surprised that such linguistic imprecisions are among the dangers of societies such as ours:

'The most common expedient employed by democratic nations to make an innovation in language consists in giving some unwonted meaning to an expression already in use. This method is very simple, prompt, and convenient; no learning is required to use it aright, and ignorance itself rather facilitates the practice; but that practice is most dangerous to the language. . . . The consequence is that writers hardly ever appear to dwell upon a single thought, but they always seem to point their aim at a knot of ideas, leaving the reader to judge which of them has been hit.'

Such a critical examination would have the double virtue of making clear the inconsistencies and vacuity of much that has been written, and of putting new writers on their guard against the possible ambiguities of some of the abstract terms in common usage. When, for instance, an influential educationalist like John Dewey, perhaps 'the most important single factor in the progressive education movement',[1] proclaims in his *Pedagogic Creed* 'education, therefore, is a process of living and not a preparation for future living', we need to ask what precisely is meant, for it is an idea to which Dewey constantly returns. What, for instance, is a 'process of living'? What exactly does

---

[1] Joseph Ratner: Introduction to *Education To-day* by John Dewey.

20

Dewey mean by the word 'process', which is a word he uses frequently. Does it, for instance, imply a restriction on the word 'living', denote one of several possible ways of living or a means of securing some end in life (as, for instance, in the sentence 'this is one of several processes for making carbon dioxide'); or does it just mean any series of events that could take place in 'life'? Is there any shift of meaning in the word 'living' between its use in 'process of living' and in 'preparation for future living'? Would it not be possible to argue that any 'preparation for future living' involved a 'process of living'? Such is a selection of questions that might possibly be asked.

But, of course, such analysis will not proceed for long before it is found that more fundamental questions are raised. For instance, having regard to the context of Dewey's work and ideas, what I think Dewey means by the sentence quoted is something like this: 'School' and 'life' are to be regarded as co-extensive; the school is not to be looked upon as an institution which is cut off in most respects from the 'life' around it, or where the problems to be faced are different in kind from the sorts of problems that face people in the world outside, in 'real life'. Thus, for instance, children should have experience in the exercise of democratic control, because such control is a feature of the society of their time; hence the need for school parliaments and the like. Moreover, the sort of experience that children get in running such parliaments will be the same kind of experience that adults get in running their parliaments.

If this is accepted as a reasonably accurate paraphrase, does in fact convey something of what Dewey intended to convey, we need then to go on to ask if Dewey's observation is in fact true. Is the school (or should the school be) as Dewey describes it, or is it (or should it be) a special type of institution, adapted to the needs and requirements of individuals who because of age, tend to differ biologically and psychologically from adults? Are, in fact, the problems of children's parliaments sufficiently like those encountered in adult parliaments to justify Dewey's contention? Should children be encouraged in the sort of egotistical self-inflation that the exercise of such control and the consequent diminished role of the teacher's authority might well beget?

Once questions of this sort are asked (and I give only a small selection of some that might be asked) issues will be raised that far transcend the original query. The whole problem of the relationship between the school and society is involved. Are, for instance, political notions (in this case, of democracy), which may well be admitted to be desirable in the task of governing the community at large, relevant to the sort of society that a school is? After all, a school *is* a particular type of social entity, and its aims and ends may be said, in certain respects at least, to differ from the ends and aims of society at large. A school, for instance, is specifically concerned with learning in a way in which society at large is not. This, I think, will be admitted. Are such notions of democracy admissible in a world where learning is one of the primary ends, where, in fact, in the estimation of many people, it should be the primary end? After all, the rightness or wrongness of an arithmetical sum cannot be decided by a show of hands; nor is the relative value of the various disciplines of learning to be decided by majority vote (though writers like Dewey explicitly deny that there is a hierarchy of value as between the various subjects). Then, of course, the problem of the teacher's authority is raised. The teacher is in a particular position; he is not appointed by the children, and he is appointed because he knows much more about his subject than the children do. Thus his authority, which in part, at least, derives from his subject (I am assuming his competence) cannot be called into question. If he says that the Battle of Hastings took place in 1066, it must be accepted; no dictate of the sternest tyrant could be more absolute. Thus, while learning is a matter of any importance in our schools, the teacher can never quite be reduced to the role of Big Friend or Cheer Leader, as seems to be the modern ambition.[1]

Thus questions of value and authority have been raised, and

[1] Cf. *Projects and their Place in Education* by Jean M. A. Armstrong; where the teacher is told to 'give a five-minute pep talk at intervals to rouse interest and enthusiasm'.

thus ultimate questions cannot be avoided; for one's answers to such problems will be intimately bound up with one's fundamental views on the nature of man and his relationship to the universe, of which society is only an element. And such problems are properly the province of the theologian and the philosopher, and to solve them demands the most serious attention of which man is capable.

I trust it will not seem that there is anything fantastic in this long chain which leads from the minutiae of classroom management to the ultimate problems of man; for indeed, the way we behave in particular situations, the sort of learning we advocate, the nature of the relationship we encourage as between teacher and taught, the way in which we organize our schools, and the ends which we expect them to subserve, in fact the whole complex part played by those multifarious activities, to which we give the name 'education', in the total life of man, will be intimately bound up with the answers we give to just such ultimate problems.

When, therefore, I make a plea for more attention to the problems of educational philosophy, I am not urging something that is remote, and in the pejorative sense of that ill-used word, 'academic'; I am urging something that is immediately and intimately the concern of all teachers, and especially those who are engaged in training teachers. Day after day, in the classroom and in the lecture hall we tender advice and give counsel that a little more careful thought would perhaps show to be ill-conceived and mistaken. Moreover many teachers themselves are sorely puzzled, in this time of revolution, as to where the truth lies. As Professor Butterfield has said, 'Amongst historians, as in other fields, the blindest of all the blind are those who are unable to examine their own presuppositions, and blithely imagine therefore that they do not possess any'; and he adds the warning, 'It must be emphasized that we create tragedy after tragedy for ourselves by a lazy unexamined doctrine of man which is current amongst us and which the study of history does not support.' It is a warning to be heeded.

The question is, where is one to look even for an airing of the problems touched upon. Enormous numbers of people in the educational world are engaged on the details of technique and method or on the psychology of the learning process, work the value of which varies a great deal from individual to individual, but some part of which is vitiated because the question as to what this vast array of particularized information is intended to subserve is so rarely asked; vitiated, too, because much of it springs from conceptions about human nature that are naïve and, as Professor Butterfield points out, unhistorical. The enormous stranglehold which the young and still presumptuous science of psychology has obtained and the introduction of political notions into spheres where they do not apply created the sort of situation against which Newman so rightly inveighed in his lectures on the university:

'. . . no science whatever, however comprehensive it may be, but will fall largely into error, if it be constituted the sole exponent of all things in heaven and earth, and that, for the simple reason that it is encroaching on territory not its own, and undertaking problems which it has no instruments to solve.'

Philosophy needs all the aid she can get from the other sciences; and what the psychologist and the politician have to say has its relevance; but final ends are the province of the philosopher and without adequate ends the most accomplished learning technique the world can offer is but a vanity.

At a time when individual autonomy in cultural and educational matters has reached catastrophic proportions, when the anarchy that Arnold prophesied is with us daily, when, to continue in the words of F. H. Bradley, which are even more relevant to-day than they were when they were written seventy-five years ago,

'. . . all have opinions, and too many also practice of their own; when every man knows better, and does worse, than his father before him; when to be enlightened is to be possessed by some wretched theory, which is our own just so far as it separates us from others; and to be cultivated is to be aware that doctrine means narrowness, that all truths are so true that any truth must be false; when "young pilgrims", at their outset, are "spoiled by the sophistry" of shallow moralities, and the fruit of life rots as it ripens . . .'[1]

one of the main purposes of the essays which follow is to explore the 'philosophic'[2] grounds for a reassertion of the notion of authority in our educational and cultural concerns. On some such reassertion, in terms which it will be part of the purpose of this book to determine, depends the *quality* of our freedom. It is astonishing how quickly those who speak of the necessity of authority lay themselves open to charges of neo-fascism, 'authoritarianism' and other imputations of a like nature. It is equally odd that the upholders of 'freedom' are rarely accused of nihilism or anarchism. This is partly because we are emotionally attuned to receive the notion of 'freedom'—without thought about the ends this freedom is to subserve—whereas the notion of authority has to overcome a deep-seated emotional prejudice. It is, however, the *nature* of the authority invoked which should decide the degree of repugnance or acceptance with which it is received. Obviously, we cannot accept any and every manifestation of authority; indeed, the sort of authority which in our social and economic life we are accepting seems likely to involve culturally unfortunate repercussions.

The authority which I am considering is the true source of 'freedom'—that higher freedom which reasserts the dignity and

---

[1] F. H. Bradley: *Ethical Studies.*

[2] 'By *meditation*, rather than by *observation*? And by the latter in consequence of the former? As eyes, for which the former has predetermined their field of vision, and to which, as to its organ, it communicates a microscopic power.' (Coleridge: *Biographia Literaria*, Chapter XVIII.) I use the word 'philosophic' somewhat in the Coleridgean manner, rather than in the strict technical sense. For Coleridge expresses the insight of an artist who is also a 'thinker'; and the combination of the two provides, to my mind, one of the most valuable forms of 'philosophy'. Cf. too, A. N. Whitehead: 'I hold that philosophy is the critic of abstractions. Its function is the double one, first of harmonizing them by assigning to them their right relative status as abstractions, and secondly of completing them by direct comparison with more concrete intuitions of the universe, and thereby promoting the formation of more complete schemes of thought. It is in respect to this comparison

worth of man. It is no mechanical, static thing, as I hope to make clear, but a living, dynamic principle of a tradition of objective learning reinvoked and reabsorbed. If it turns out to be no precisely determined matter of checks and balances, is not, in fact, another of those mechanistic 'blue-prints' for living which are the misfortune of our age, it is because my notion of authority is intended to transcend those comparatively crude and insufficient political manifestations which are never subtle enough to embody any vital living principle of being.

First, the implications of the new 'group' approach to social and political problems will be examined; they will take us to a consideration of education under planning and the sorts of cultural values that one of the most famous of the advocates of planning displays. The older movement towards individual self-expression will then be re-assessed and what appear to be some of its deficiencies revealed. The more positive part of the book will involve an examination of the educational and cultural ideas of Arnold, Newman and Lawrence; these, it is hoped, will point the way to a profounder sense of the true relationship between freedom and order. Finally, the claims and nature of authority in education will be explicitly examined.

At least three things, it is hoped, will emerge from the book: the need to consider very much more carefully than many educationalists seem to think necessary the implications of the terms in common use; the need to transcend many of the superficial social and educational ideas of the day if the relative

that the testimony of great poets is of such importance. Their survival is evidence that they express deep intuitions of mankind penetrating into what is universal in concrete fact. Philosophy is not one among the sciences with its own little scheme of abstractions which it works away at perfecting and improving. It is the survey of sciences, with the special objects of their harmony, and of their completion. It brings to this task, not only the evidence of the separate sciences, but also its own appeal to concrete experience. It confronts the sciences with concrete fact.' (*Science and the Modern World*, Chapter V.) As Coleridge with poetry, so I with education do not think we can progress far without 'a *philosophic* (and inasmuch as it is actualized by an effort of freedom, an *artificial*) consciousness, which lies beneath or (as it were) *behind* the spontaneous consciousness natural to all reflective beings'. (*Biographia Literaria*, Chapter XII.)

claims of the individual's self-development as against those of the necessary discipline implied in the body of human learning are to be met harmoniously; and the importance of what the literary artist has to say on education.

CHAPTER TWO

PLANNING AND POPULARIZATION

*'Culture is always assigning to system-makers and systems
a smaller share in the bent of human destiny than their friends
like.'*

— MATTHEW ARNOLD: *Culture and Anarchy*

[I]

The late Professor Karl Mannheim set out certain
views on the possibilities of mass education in a short
pamphlet published as a Supplement to a *Christian
News Letter*,[1] entitled *The Meaning of Popularization in
a Mass Society*. This essay is admittedly brief; yet it contains a
succinct statement on one of the major educational problems
of our age by an educationalist of great repute, the problem of
the dilution of value in a mass society, the problem implicit
in the notion of 'mass civilization and minority culture', as
Dr. F. R. Leavis has expressed it. Thus a close examination of
the views Professor Mannheim here expressed is worth undertaking. For the assumptions on which Professor Mannheim has
based his cultural and social ideas are ones which, partly due to
his influence, perhaps, are popular in certain circles to-day;
nevertheless they reveal a reliance on habits of thought that in
some ways might appear to have outlived their usefulness. An

---

[1] No. 227. I have chosen to restrict my scope of attack because this pamphlet gives me the opportunity for detailed and close analysis; with the
wider issues of *Ideology and Utopia* I am not here concerned. In this pamphlet,
too, Prof. Mannheim makes some of his few explicitly artistic and cultural
judgements, with which I am so much concerned. What they reveal seems to
me significant.

examination, therefore, of limited elements of Professor Mannheim's theories may help us to understand important features of
a type of mind that, despite its insufficiency, is exerting an increasing and, to my mind, somewhat baneful influence on our
daily lives. I am also anxious to bring out Professor Mannheim's
cultural views because it seems to me that certain intellectual
circles are accepting the social conditions of planning and all
that it entails without realizing that these changes may have
repercussions that would be culturally unfortunate. It may be
that in the conflict of loyalties 'culture' will have to go by the
board; but it is as well to realize something of what is likely to
happen.

First it is necessary to consider Professor Mannheim in a
wider context. For Professor Mannheim occupied an influential
position. Formerly Professor of Sociology in the University of
Frankfurt-on-Main, he was connected for a time with the
London School of Economics and then became Professor of
Education at the University of London. He brought with him
habits of thought derived from a mental atmosphere somewhat
different from that to be found in this country. It is an atmosphere whose characteristic thought movement is from the
general to the particular, one which tends to ignore the petti-
fogging details of 'the stubborn and irreducible' facts of nature
at the behest of a more grandiose mental conception of the ideal.
It is a viewpoint sanctioned by the Kantian distinction between the empirical and the rational ego. This division (in
much German thought) between the outer realm of action and
the inner realm of consciousness has led to that fundamental
imbalance between the lessons derived from the experience
which the great technical efficiency of the Germans has provided (where all is mechanical obedience, subordination and
discipline), and those gained from a feeling of spiritual freedom,
of complete intellectual self-determination in the mental sphere.
Hence, perhaps—to translate into a common, and because common, significant metaphor—the nation of sleep-walkers, though
sleep-walkers whose dreams follow a similar pattern; and hence
the incompatibility of the sleep-walker in the domain of the

29

shop-keeper, whose characteristic philosophical expression, from that close association with everyday material objects that buying and selling imply, and from a contemplation of those general laws that the 'state of the market' impels on the attention, lies more in a certain practicality. Yet we are at present witnessing, through the hospitality so rightly extended to foreign refugees, the bringing to bear of just such an alien tradition that serves to stimulate, as all new ways of thought are stimulating, but one which contains certain dangers unless we realize fully the implications of these new assumptions of use and wont.[1]

For Professor Mannheim was one of the chief exponents of planning in this country, and through his own works—particularly his *Man and Society*, published h~re in 1940—and his general editorship of Kegan Paul's International Library of Sociology and Social Reconstruction, was concerned to persuade us of the necessity of taking this step for the preservation of our way of life. Of course Professor Mannheim was not the first and only planner, and the influence, pervasive throughout the 'thirties and increasingly important much earlier, of the rigid systematized thinking of the German Marx, had already prepared many of the intellectuals to listen sympathetically to other thinkers of a similar tendency. Now a plan[2] (a word

[1] This contrast, admittedly based on popular generalizations about national character very properly suspect, nevertheless by its very persistence seems to point to certain endemic qualities to be found in the two nations. The Germans themselves have not been backward in admitting its truth.

[2] I am only concerned, as I have said, in a book dealing specifically with education, to subject the small pamphlet quoted above to detailed analysis, and these remarks on planning must be taken in a generalized sense, though they refer to certain features of Professor Mannheim's own schemes. I believe, however, that the whole of Professor Mannheim's work on planning would repay analysis of the type to which the late Professor Susan Stebbing subjected the work of Professors Jeans and Eddington, and E. H. Carr. This, however, would provide matter for another book. Here I can only commend to the attention the chapter which Professor Mannheim would no doubt regard as an adequate reply to my strictures. It appears in *Man and Society* and is called 'Real understanding of freedom a prelude to action' (cf. the comment on the use of the word 'real' below). There we are urged to forgo 'the luxury of arbitrary interference' (note the emotively charged words to describe what we would at present refer to as our 'freedom') to attain a 'higher level of freedom' as a result of a contract to establish the plan. But

closely associated with military and scientific operations, where the relevant factors are reasonably confined, the resources capable of rational assessment and where there is an immediate, restricted and clearly apprehensible end in view) is always the work of the conscious intellect abstracting from the totality of existence certain only of its characteristics, and seeking on a basis of this abstract conception of reality to realize certain ends. These ends can only be achieved by imposition of means of varying degrees of incompatibility with the living organisms that are the objects of the planner's concern. That any *rigid* attempt[1] thus to impose means in the larger field of the totality of human society must prove incompatible in this way is certain because no human mind, nor any set of human minds, however able, can adequately assess those imponderables which escape the notice of the cognitive ego in its conscious attempt to fixate the conditions and limitations of being. Even in military matters where, as I say, the end seems to be quite clearly understandable —the need to defeat the enemy—the plan may—and in fact on one side, must—go astray, if not immediately, at any rate (as in the case of Hannibal) in its further consequences. Even the conception of the end in view is subject, of course, to the individual limitations of the planners because of the ultimate imperfection of the human mind. It is perhaps a sign of the inadequacy of Professor Mannheim's outlook that it was not until a friend pointed it out to him that he appears to have realized the existence of the problem, 'Who is to plan the planners?'

the establishment of such a plan as Professor Mannheim had in mind seems to me to lead inevitably, despite all the grand talk about 'higher level of freedom', to the type of situation discussed in the later part of this chapter. Even in Professor Mannheim's own analysis, freedom merely appears as an item in the plan, i.e. we shall apparently be directed when and where to be 'free' ('freedom can only be secured by *direction from the key points*' ! Op. cit., p. 379—my italics). It is hard not to be sceptical.

[1] I must stress my depreciation of the rigidity involved, for obviously, in view of what follows, I do not wish this to be taken as an attack on *all* possibilities of rational assessment. Yet planning in a planned society involves, as we shall see, a *very* high degree of abstraction, and the attempt to order the almost infinite complexity of human nature in this way seems to me catastrophic for the higher human values.

Any plan will, in fact, bear witness ultimately to just those values that the planners think desirable. It is characteristic, too, that when Professor Mannheim, in the pamphlet referred to above, turns to define those groups which are to be the sources of original inspiration, the leaders of the dynamic society—presumably the planners themselves—he has to confess that they 'constitute a class which is hardly capable of scientific definition'. And then, more revealingly still, he admits that 'there is no objective measurement that can be applied, and the judgement depends largely upon the personal valuation of the observer'—a statement which seems to me to destroy the basis of Professor Mannheim's activities; for we are once more thrown back on the 'chaos' (as Professor Mannheim conceives it) of the liberal era, depending on the clash of individual or group valuations with the additional disadvantage that whichever group comes out on top is presumably to impose its views on the rest. Moreover, such values as the planners can conceive are, if Professor Mannheim's writings are any indication, on a high level of abstraction. The argument is conducted always on an abstract plane, and the metaphors he employs are frequently derived from science, mechanical things ('mechanism' is a favourite word) and military tactics. A plan, of course, must involve thinking of people in terms of labelled groups, and of the individual only in accordance with those abstract qualities that make him the member of a group, just as a military commander thinks of his men according to their technical capacity as fighting men and not as lovers, fathers, writers of poems, nor as possessing other vital characteristics of living, developing, organic human beings. Any plan, in fact, implies the imposition of something dead—because abstract and preconceived—on the living organism. Once the attempt is made to put the plan into operation in all its unavoidable rigidity, the attitude of the planner must be that of Procrustes or else his plan breaks down. Admittedly a certain amount of improvisation may be possible, and to give him his due, it is obvious that Professor Mannheim was anxious to preserve what he called 'democratic freedom'. What he does not appear to have seen is that the planner is bound up with the logic of his own position. Once improvisation passes a certain mark the plan disappears and the end in view suffers a considerable mutation: we are then back, in fact, in the old *laissez-faire* habit of patching, which is just what the planner wishes to avoid. Improvisation, therefore, is only possible within certain strict limits, however well-intentioned the planner may be. Professor Mannheim expresses it:

'It (i.e. planning) is not the treatment of symptoms but an attack on the strategic points, fully realizing the result.'

The clinical and military metaphors are significant and the satisfying sense of a comprehensiveness in assault which can so easily degenerate into ruthlessness, is to be noted. It is however just that inability of the human mind to assess fully the result that vitiates the planner's claim to omniscience.

Again, it is interesting to note that the planner adds one more to those schemes of a material Utopia that have replaced the older idea of pie-in-the-sky by the promise of a whole pastry-cook's shop round the corner at the price of submission to the impersonality of the plan. A further aspect of the plan's appeal lies in the fact that it is associated with that wish to control the future which has been one of the most potent manifestations in Western thought of the individual's desire to perpetuate himself against the disintegration of time. But in this case there is a significant twist; the individual finds his protection in the future of the community and in the anonymity which that implies; responsibility for the future is pushed on to the impersonal forces involved in the proper working of society that the plan implies, and is to a considerable extent removed from the care of the individual. It is interesting, though perhaps a trifle unfair to Professor Mannheim, to compare the planner's brand of futurity with that of the Macbeths. Lady Macbeth also had the same desire to grasp the future:

> *Thy letters have transported me beyond*
> *This ignorant present, and I feel now*
> *The future in the instant.*

Now this conquest of the future can be conceived of in two ways; at the one extreme the individual can assert his individual ego at the expense of the 'natural' order of the community, which is Macbeth's way; or by a process of seeing things only in the abstract he can seek to sink his individualism in that of the artificially created group and persuade himself that his identity is best preserved by contact with it. Hence the popularity to-day of the various social ' 'isms', in most cases accepted because of a desire to shift the responsibility of individual conduct on to the impersonal processes of the social mechanism. In Shakespeare's day there still existed a more 'natural' order, 'more natural' because based on the rhythms of the seasons and of the crops in a community still primarily agricultural in its being, by which to judge the disintegrating effect of the assertion of the individual will; but now it is impossible to conceive of the sinking of the individual in the purely man-made and mechanical conception of the planner's community without seeing in such a project a definite regression. There is no escape from the burden of self-consciousness which three centuries of individual assertion have brought about, by the planner's attempt to identify his will with that of the community and to assure the future on the basis of the anonymity—flatteringly termed 'integration'—that such an identification implies. For both the plan and the acceptance of the plan are the products of an age which feels its fundamental insecurity and turns aside from the fullness of life at the behest of the clearly defined but rigid. Such phenomena are related to the rise to power of the bureaucrat—a manifestation which is at once a cause and a symptom of the increasing mechanization of life and of the impersonality of human relationships. Hence the continual complaint among intellectuals of a lack of vitality (no longer a bang but a whimper) of which the extreme expression in the upper reaches of society is the necrophilia of people like Dali and among the lower-middle class is the cult of violence—the method of self-assertion adopted by the fundamentally insecure—implied in fascism and communism. It is chiefly because the English body politic, partly no doubt because of its insularity, has succeeded in retaining a certain *organic* (as opposed to a mechanical and imposed) quality of interrelated social obligations[1] that planning is less popular here than elsewhere.

But there are one or two other interesting features of the planner's dream of the future which merit consideration before we turn more particularly to those educational plans of Professor Mannheim's that are to materialize his vision of the new community. Professor Mannheim postulates a 'dynamic' society. Convention he regards as stultifying; his outlook implies ever a reaching out towards the socially new, and he looks upon the 'continual emergence of groups who will originate dominant ideas and form or change the sensibility of their time' as desirable.

This emphasis on the new—which incidentally is curiously at odds with other features of Professor Mannheim's thought, as we shall see later—no doubt is meant to provide the obverse side to that lack of individual responsibility which submission to a plan implies. What society lacks in depth it is to make up in movement. Now, of course, it is perfectly true that societies do become fossilized; and there is always a danger that life will become stereotyped and conventional. Nevertheless it is the emphasis that Professor Mannheim places on the idea of continual change and the *naïveté* of his approval of an endless series of mutations that invite condemnation. Conventions of conduct and morality sum up, in the sphere of the imponderables, the wisdom of the race and are not to be abandoned lightly. They provide a certain atmosphere of emotional security, which is necessary to all development, and which comes from a sense of being in right relationship to established rhythms of life. It is one of the great faults of our present-day urban scientific civilization that the rate of change and the mobility of population is so great that the individual has no time to draw strength from the embodied wisdom which forms tradition; for tradition is the result of growth and implies a relationship of a very different sort from the mechanically imposed community of the planner. Tradition can, of course, be stultifying and cramping, for life must be lived forwards and not backwards; yet it can only be lived for-

[1] Cp. the English eighteenth-century aristocracy with the French.

wards satisfactorily in terms of the experience gained from the past (though at the same time, it may be added in parenthesis that, paradoxically enough, experience gained from the past is never adequate to enable the individual to assess completely the requirements of the future). Hence the need of change; but hence the need of a change adequately related to experience gained from, and based on a respect for the past, the past history of the race. Indeed, this continual grasping after the new, as Shakespeare realized, related as it is to the desire of futurity examined earlier, is always a characteristic of a *lack of being* whether at an individual or a communal level. Macbeth, in seeking to assert his individual ego against the traditional relationships of respect to his king, suffers throughout the play a progressive loss of being which in the end takes from him even 'the taste of fears', makes life an endless succession of to-morrows without meaning, and turns him into the 'dwarfish thief' whom Malcolm's forces so contemptuously seek out. And here Shakespeare symbolically reveals that only those who can draw nutriment from established relationships are capable of full development. It is Macbeth's rejection of Duncan's offer, expressed metaphorically in terms of *natural growth* and development—

> *I have begun to plant thee, and will labour*
> *To make thee full of growing*

—that leads to his downfall. Professor Mannheim, whose mechanical outlook is in direct contradiction of all that wisdom has previously found satisfying, reflects the growing impersonality of human relationships.

The ground is now prepared for a closer investigation of one aspect of Professor Mannheim's outlook—that with which we are here concerned—his attitude towards education. In his view, if a mass-planned society is to be anything but a society of termites, education must play an important part in fitting the individual to respond to the new ways of thought discussed above. An analysis of his suggestions may show us more fully the reasons which lie behind the inadequacy of his views. His ideas on education can well be judged from this extract from *Man and Society*:

'Sociologists do not regard education solely as a means of realizing abstract ideas of culture, such as humanism or technical specialization, but as part of the process of influencing men and women. *Education can only be understood when we know for what society and for what social position the pupils are being educated. Education does not mould men in the abstract but in and for a given society.*'

So much for the view that the aim of education involves the development of the potentialities of the individual. Whatever Professor Mannheim thinks the sentences in italics mean, and however much he may protest that such is not his aim, it is not difficult to see how an education preconceived in such a manner can easily degenerate into propaganda for a particular type of society. It has to be admitted that even in the most liberal view the development of the individual is bound to be restricted by the preconceptions derived both by the teacher and the taught, partly from the limitations of the individual mind, and partly from the influence of the environment. All notions of 'being' are set in a particular context, and freedom must always be relative, as can be seen from what has been said above about the healthy features of traditional modes of conduct; its incidence raises such questions as freedom from and for what? But to make only one aspect of the individual—his social—the ultimate criterion of value is not only to make man the end and aim of all things, but is also to rely on a singularly restricted view of the nature of that man. For a man is an individual as well as a social being; and outside himself he has duties to a super-personal set of values as well as to other people. A man must always be prepared to accept a certain amount of responsibility for the conduct of others, because of a sense both of obligation and of charity. Nevertheless there seem to be limits beyond which the individual's responsibility does not and must not, for the sake of his integrity, go. The fact that that limit is extremely difficult to define does not seem to me to be an adequate excuse for shirking the responsibility.

37

It is not difficult to see that Professor Mannheim makes out a superficially attractive case for mass education by appealing to certain prejudices that are likely to evoke an enthusiastic response from many educational circles to-day. First comes the attack on superior persons—in the pamphlet quoted—equated with 'closed academic circles', who appear to favour 'an artificial clumsiness', and who cultivate an 'academic aloofness which finds life sublime only in a kind of stratosphere when our minds are kept safely at a distance from suffering and vulgarity'. It would take too long to discover to what extent these academic circles are fictions of Professor Mannheim's imagination. A visitor to this year's exhibition at the Royal Academy might tend to favour the general direction of Professor Mannheim's attack; nevertheless there are academic circles as keenly alive intellectually as any others to be found; and the whole attack on the academic is to be deprecated as part of that movement which acclaims the superficial and irresponsible and which is so debasing the standards of our time.

But to continue with Professor Mannheim's views on the nature of those who are responsible for our cultural heritage. Culture (he uses the word, I take it, in much of the Arnoldian sense; at least he wants all to share the same basic culture) is not to be the prerogative of the educated few; and though the original thinker is to play an important part in the evolution of our dynamic society he desires that new truths, new ideas should be accessible to all; only so can the society become integrated. What happens, I wonder, to the original thinker who does not think in concordance with the dictates of the society and of the social position he occupies? Hence the necessity of popularization, of a type that will not merely provide a 'dilution of real substance', but be a 'creative dissemination'. The whole problem, indeed, resolves itself into the 'dissemination of the substance of culture without diluting it'.

Of these creative disseminators, these who 'originate at lower levels', Professor Mannheim gives several examples which it will be instructive to examine later. For the moment it is necessary to look at the distinction mentioned above between 'culture' and the 'substance of culture'. Professor Mannheim recommends a process by which this creative dissemination is to take place. It involves fastening on to what is essential—a democratizing process that is

'a search for truth that is in principle accessible to everybody, not because it is trivial or diluted, but because it is reduced to the really human elements of knowledge.'

What do certain of these phrases mean? Truth, for instance, or such elements of truth as man's mind can encompass, is always in principle accessible to everybody provided they have the mental capacity to grasp the 'truth' that is presented to them; here, the words, if they convey anything at all, merely fog the issue. It is not a question of whether the truth in principle is there to be grasped, but whether the type of people Professor Mannheim has in mind are in fact capable of grasping it. Then what are the *really human* elements in knowledge? All the elements in knowledge are human (except, possibly, the religious would argue, those elements based on revelation: but I do not think that that is the contrast Professor Mannheim has in mind); for they are the products of human intelligence in its relationship to what exists outside the human mind, the Object (human and non-human). In so far as the words quoted above have any meaning, they appear to be purely emotive—to give a warm comforting sense of togetherness in contrast to that academic aloofness of which Professor Mannheim so strongly disapproves. The word 'real' too, is a stumbling-block in all this sort of writing. In a recently contemporary journal (*Pilot Papers*), Mr. Jarvis, in an article on *Discussion Groups*, quotes this passage with approval, and states that

'Adult education for democracy ought to concern itself with the real contemporary problems of real people.'

How does one qualify to become a *real* person with a *real* problem? The only way it is possible to give it a meaning is to make it refer to

'the type of person of whom I socially approve interested in the sort of problem I regard as important.'

Its aim however is to gain approval; in an age that is so loosely pragmatic in its outlook as our own, the sense of being in touch with what the writer conceives to be 'reality' which the use of the word 'real' (and 'contemporary') here gives, conveys a comforting impression of concern for immediate issues, more satisfying to a certain type of mind than a more careful definition of the issues involved would be.

Previously, however, Professor Mannheim has given a clue to the origin of this idea of the 'essential':

'Descartes, for example, in his treatise on method suggests the need for getting away from the complexity of scholastic discussion and the dogmatism of closed groups. He made it a criterion for the new type of thought that it should be clear and distinct.'

We have already seen that Professor Mannheim associates himself, in his emphasis on the new, with a type of anti-historicism that is in fact typically Cartesian. Descartes, in fact, comes at the beginning of that tendency to abstraction which is associated with the scientific revolution. Certain features only in a totality presented are seized upon and in those elements the 'real' as opposed to the fictitious qualities 'accidentally' associated with them are seen. Descartes asserts the power of the cognitive ego—*cogito ergo sum*—and makes the abstractions of the cognitive ego the basis of the identity of the individual. It is the work of people like Descartes—and, despite differences of method, of Bacon, too—that gives the truth to Nietzsche's remark that the Lutheran Reformation was the indignation of the simple against the complex.[1] Such a process of simplification is inherent in the scientific outlook, for at least in its earlier stages science involved a surrender of the complexity of the rationalizing intellect (as that was understood in the Middle Ages) to requirements imposed by the urge to investigate certain elements only abstracted from the material world presented

[1] Descartes, of course, was an orthodox Catholic, but his philosophical work is spiritually akin to the revolt that Luther represents against the complexity of the mediaeval outlook.

to the mind. When Descartes conducted his experiment with the wax, he found what he thought was the 'essential' element connecting the hard wax with the melted. What he did not see was that that 'essential' element was only the essential element for certain purposes; those qualities of hardness, yellowness, etc., which the wax possessed under certain external conditions of temperature, etc., were just as 'real' as the idea of the wax which he arrived at by comparing the hard and the molten wax. The same process can be examined in the changed attitude towards language which Professor L. C. Knights, in an interesting essay on Bacon, based on Mr. T. S. Eliot's remark about the 'dissociation of sensibility' that set in during the seventeenth century, examines.[1] A comparison of the Shakespearean and the Baconian use of metaphor shows the difference between a use of language springing from the awareness of the interrelated quality of the various planes of human existence, and one that denotes the dominance of certain aspects of the mind—especially of the assertive will and of the calculating intellect working towards limited ends assessable in terms of 'practical' politics —over the rest. Bacon's metaphors and similes are, indeed, purely illustrative; the points of contact do not create an awareness in the mind of any possible modes of relationship but merely result from the realization of certain abstract similarities between the 'tenor' and the 'vehicle' which will serve to illustrate a meaning already completely formed. As Professor Knights expresses it:

'. . . the whole trend of Bacon's work is to encourage the relegation of instinctive and emotional life to a sphere separate from and inferior to the sphere of thought and practical activity.'

This long aside on Bacon and Descartes has been worth while because it shows the beginning of a process that has led directly to Professor Mannheim's educational theories. The aims—those of control and mastery over the environment—are the same. The temper of mind is similar; even Professor Mann-

[1] L. C. Knights: Bacon and the Seventeenth-century Dissociation of Sensibility, *Explorations*, Chatto and Windus, 1946.

heim's style exemplifies what three centuries of Cartesian abstraction can do. The whole of his view on popularization, based as it is on an entirely fictitious relationship between 'knowledge' and the 'essentials' of knowledge, stands revealed as a further example of that process of abstraction which Descartes applied to his piece of wax. For as soon as we start reducing anything to its essentials, we have to ask ourselves 'essential for what purpose?' Yellowness and hardness may well be the essential qualities of wax if our interests are those of a painter. Any idea which is stated in different, simpler terms becomes immediately a different idea; it may bear some relationship to the statement of the original idea, just as requests framed in the form of 'Please be quiet' and 'Shut up' bear some relationship to an expressed desire for tranquillity. But there is a whole world of difference between the emotional context of the two clauses, a difference which is just as real as the relationship of the two to a third impersonal translation. It is precisely because he tends to think on a certain level of abstraction that Professor Mannheim makes the mistake of imagining that any idea can be reduced to a simpler form than that in which it already exists and *still remain the same undiluted idea*. It is, of course, frequently possible to break up propositions about the nature of human existence and the requirements of man into a number of simpler elements for the purpose of examining each element in detail; but to mistake any one of those simplifications for the essential serves only to betray the nature of the interest of the person directing the scrutiny, unless such a simplification is backed by the prevailing emphasis of the originator of the idea; and even then, no idea can ever truly be stated in any other terms but those in which it has been first formulated; varying degrees of approximation are alone possible, though admittedly necessary for the purpose of argument.

When we turn to examine those examples of the substance of culture which Professor Mannheim gives, any remaining doubts about the inadequacy of his cultural judgements are dispelled. His remarks about jazz—an example he gives of the possibilities of popularization—are too obscure to admit of discussion, though the manner in which he concedes the necessity of an appeal to a connoisseur for the purpose of distinguishing the 'work of routine' from the genuine 'ecstasy' seems to me, if it means what it appears to mean, to give his case away. His other example of 'creativity' at a lower level is Noel Coward, who apparently ' . . . conveys a new type of vibration to a simpler type of mind . . .' and is not to be considered as a '. . . publicity agent for those who create on a higher plane'.

We may well absolve Mr. Coward from the latter charge, for there is nothing in his work that shows even the slightest awareness of the work of those who create on a higher plane. It is still more difficult to discover the precise nature of the 'new' vibration Mr. Coward is supposed to convey to any mind at all. Far from being an originator, he is content to reinforce, in his capacity as paid entertainer, whose function it is to give the public what it wants, the prejudices of his audience. To state that his work gives us '. . . the same unexpected shock which undermines our complacency when we enjoy great art or listen to a great orator . . .' provides a measure by which we can judge the depth of Professor Mannheim's appreciation of artistic seriousness.[1]

Nor is it sufficient to appeal to mediaeval times as providing a precedent for the capacity to express a common experience at a number of levels, for the situations of mediaeval and modern man are quite different in several important respects, as can be deduced from what has been said above. The mediaeval age had a unifying principle that lay outside the social order, but even so it is useless to imagine that the theologian and the peasant paid homage to the same God or that any mediaeval theologian would have been muddle-headed enough to imagine that the peasant had somehow seized upon the 'essential' feature of the God that he worshipped.[2] The difference, which may partly explain Professor Mannheim's approach, lies in the fact

[1] This, of course, is not meant to deny that Mr. Coward has talent of a certain type. The particular type, and the reason for its popularity, would repay investigation.

[2] The comment of William Blake to the effect that the fool sees not the same tree as a wise man is relevant here.

that the mediaeval peasant was not in a position to impose his views on the rest of society as his modern counterpart, the urban proletarian, in a mass social order, is capable of doing; for it is hard to avoid the conclusion that Professor Mannheim is subconsciously rationalizing a state of affairs that, once political power has been placed in the hands of those not conspicuously capable of undertaking the responsibility, as it now has, can only be made endurable by sentimentalizing the nature of these forces which are faced with the necessity of achieving some sort of order in the present chaos. Professor Mannheim's views are in fact symptomatic of a period that has sought relief from the complexity of living and from the tensions of the age by the creation of new, simplified, *social* mythologies; the nineteenth-century myth of the noble savage has been replaced by the myth of the noble scion of the masses who is to provide us with those expressions of genuineness, spontaneity, dynamism, creativity, originality and all those other qualities which, conceived in the sort of way in which they are normally conceived, the superficial taste of our age finds so desirable—

What god, man, or hero
Shall I place a tin wreath upon!

Professor Mannheim, for all the scientific colouring of his writing, all too frequently utters the sentiments and employs the stale vocabulary of our outworn romantics who, symptomatically, find 'ecstasy' one of their highest words of praise.

It is interesting to note a significant relationship between the inadequacy of Professor Mannheim's views on culture, displayed in this admittedly limited context, and the abstractness, the lack of concrete understanding of people as people, instead of as social units, which marks his social theorizing. A concern for, and the understanding of, what constitutes cultural health is perhaps an essential pre-requisite to a profounder understanding of social processes; and it is significant that in a relative consideration of Mr. Eliot and Professor Mannheim, the poet's social criticism should go deeper and appreciate the essential elements more fully than the social mechanic's.

Mr. Eliot's views on the relationship of culture and society, as he reveals them particularly in *Notes Towards the Definition of Culture*, provide something of a standard by which to judge Professor Mannheim. In that book Mr. Eliot is chiefly concerned, not with an attempt to prescribe the means by which a self-conscious 'culture' (in Arnold's sense of the self-cultivation of the individual) may be acquired, but with defining those general social conditions, in the absence of which a high state of culture is unlikely to exist. Few in our day have better credentials for the task. To him, that society is likely to achieve a high state of culture which permits at once the differentiation and the inter-communication of its people, as between their various classes, regions and sects. Thus he replaces the abstract notion of equality by the concrete realization of essential differentiation. 'It is a recurrent theme of this essay, that a people should be neither too united nor too divided, if its culture is to flourish.'

Thus, too, 'Neither a classless society nor a society of strict and impenetrable social barriers is good; each class should have constant additions and defections; the classes, while remaining distinct, should be able to mix freely; and they should all have a community of culture with each other which will give them something in common, more fundamental than the community which each class has with its counterpart in another society.'

The survival of the culture of the 'higher' class is 'dependent upon the health of the culture of the people.' Yet, '. . . Even if these conditions with which I am concerned seem to the reader to represent desirable social aims, he must not leap to the conclusion that these aims can be fulfilled solely by deliberate organization.'

The planners, then, are out: the reason for this lies in the fact that '. . . culture can never be wholly conscious . . . it cannot be planned because it is also the unconscious background to our planning'.

Though it is possible to argue that Mr. Eliot, throughout his work, somewhat unduly deprecates the possibilities of self-conscious cultivation, it is only fair to remember that his 'culture' is not the 'sum of several activities, but a way of life'. The health and coherence of a culture depend to a considerable extent on the degree of *unconscious* communication that can take place among its peoples, so that in social intercourse there is an implied reference to a background of common assumptions that makes one person intelligible to another. Thus, no person who is not *of* the culture can ever hope completely to understand, intellectually, the nature of that culture. And no person who is of the culture can ever hope completely to express the culture in objective terms: 'For to understand the culture is to understand the people, and this means an imaginative understanding. Such understanding can never be complete: either it is abstract —and the essence escapes—or else it is *lived.*'

Such 'imaginative understanding' seems to me beyond the capacity of Professor Mannheim and such, indeed, provides the crux of my argument against him. It is his understanding that leads Mr. Eliot to question one of the most cherished assumptions of modern educational policy—and certainly one that lies behind Professor Mannheim's theories—the idea of equality of opportunity. To give effect to such a notion, he thinks, would lead to too great a social fluidity; it is dependent upon an 'atomic view of society'. The *élites*, thus chosen, would '. . .consist solely of individuals whose only common bond will be their professional interest: with no social cohesion, with no social continuity. They will be united only by a part, and that the most conscious part, of their personalities; they will meet like committees.'

Mr. Eliot's criticism, then, springs from a dissatisfaction with that particular brand of self-conscious rationalism which Professor Mannheim is concerned to recommend. Mr. Eliot, indeed, reminds us that we have substituted the notion of education in the abstract—purveyed through a system of education—for what should be a unified educational process of home, social environment and school. 'For the schools can transmit only a part of culture and they can only transmit this part effectively, if the outside influences, not only family and environment, but of work and play, of newsprint and spectacles and entertainment and sport are in harmony with them.' Hence, he says, 'Education in the modern sense implies a disintegrated society, in which it has come to be assumed that there must be one measure according to which everyone is educated simply more or less. Hence *Education* has become an abstraction.'

It is a mistake, he thinks, to make all members of the community share the same basic education. 'To aim to make everyone share in the appreciation of the fruits of the more conscious part of culture is to adulterate and cheapen what you give. . . . A "mass-culture" will always be a substitute culture.'

This is well worth placing against Professor Mannheim's views on mass education. Certainly it is a point of considerable importance at a time when the idea of a basic course, implied in the American comprehensive school (which has its advocates in this country) and recommended in the recent Harvard report, receives increasing attention. Even the differentiation between secondary grammar, modern and technical schools tends to be blurred by the notion inherent in any large-scale democratic society, which, by treating each man as equally capable of exercising a vote, demands implicitly that each man shall be afforded the 'education' which shall fit him for that object.[1] And as the abstract political notion of the voter, in an age when we are dominated by abstract political notions, has replaced the concrete reality of the individual human being in so many minds, it is only natural that the education so conceived should tend towards an abstract uniformity which such ideas as 'parity of esteem' have brought about, and which Professor Mannheim's notions would further encourage.

[II]

To conclude this consideration of the cultural and educational implications of 'democratic' planning, it will be useful to include a picture of how a 'planned' school is likely to operate, and to consider, in the concrete, how a too avid concern for social purpose is likely to restrict our educational endeavours. When

[1] Cf. Chapter Six, p. 159.

Chapter Three of this book appeared in its original guise as an article in *Scrutiny*, Mr. Boris Ford contributed a reply. During the course of his reply, Mr. Ford gave a picture of life and work at a Jewish school in a Palestinian settlement at Mishmar Haemek. I would like to consider Mr. Ford's account of this school, for it seems to me that the pattern that is being evolved at Mishmar Haemek is not one confined to a specific situation peculiar to Palestine. Indeed, the picture Mr. Ford presents provides a concrete indication of how Professor Mannheim's theories might conceivably work out in practice. My criticisms of Mishmar Haemek have, therefore, a wider reference than to a single Jewish school.[1] In addition, it will provide an opportunity of showing some of the dangers inherent in the new emphasis on 'group' work—even if in an admittedly extreme form.

Mr. Ford provides us with a description of the workings of the school as an example of the possibility of purposefulness within a framework of freedom. But not any and every manifestation of purposefulness is equally acceptable. The nature of the purposefulness is a vital consideration. The worth of freedom takes its significance from the quality of the order within which it exists. When Mr. Ford reveals the educational purpose of the school, it appears to be an extremely restricted social one, in terms reminiscent of Professor Mannheim's dictum, that 'Education does not mould men in the abstract but in and for a given society', quoted above:

'The main task of these schools . . . is to produce good settlers. This means more than at first appears. It means both developing the qualities that go to make a successful Settler, and also confirming the children in their wish to go back to

---

[1] At the same time, in fairness to Mr. Ford, it must be said that in a subsequent letter to *Scrutiny*, as a reply to my response to his article, he disclaims any desire to hold up Mishmar Haemek as an ideal. Nevertheless the sympathy of his reference was marked; and in any case, even if we absolve Mr. Ford personally, his picture of the school is still a significant document—despite the brevity of his visit to it. At least, the details which strike him and which he thinks worth recording, are interesting.

Settlement life at all. . . . What makes a Settler, of course, is his socialist (may one say communist?) idealism reinforced by Zionism.'

I have no desire to deprecate the achievement of Mishmar Haemek. But to make the social aspect of man the ultimate aim is to invite condemnation in the terms which I have already enunciated in this chapter. The school develops what appear on the surface to be quite admirable qualities. 'The children develop little if any desire for *self*-advancement, they think of the *group*'s advantages and success and they accept as natural a scheme of mutual assistance.' Now it is true, as I have urged, that on any human being the claim of the group has considerable validity. People must live together; and it is right that for the common good certain personal sacrifices must be made. But to crush the independence of the self, to repress or even to fail to encourage that reasonable self-assertion proper to every living creature, to condemn which would be, as Santayana says, 'to condemn life, which could not go on without it', is to impose a form of selfishness which is no less real through being disguised under a plea for social idealism. And this is a procedure inherent in the sinister idea, which Mr. Ford reports, that the group shall only learn at the pace of the slowest member. There is no reason why the learning capacity of the dullest should be adopted as the criterion, and very good reasons against it. For indeed, such a procedure would seem to involve a very short-sighted view of the type of contribution that the brighter child could make to the general group life, a contribution in which the duller could share. Nor does the curriculum inspire confidence; and Mr. Ford, for all his claim of freedom, sanctions an educational programme which appears to me of distressing rigidity. The aim of the school is to produce settlers; it is socialist (or communist) idealism combined with Zionism that produces good settlers. Hence the projects chosen by the staff and undertaken by the children not unnaturally have 'a distinctly Zionist flavour about them'. The children's learning, he asserts, 'is prompted and disciplined by their study of con-

49

crete situations and problems, with the result that it seldom seems academic'; it is 'not an end pursued for its own sake but a means to solid everyday achievement'. Now what, I wonder, provides Mr. Ford's criterion of 'solid everyday achievement'? That, I assume, which is in line with socialist-Zionist teachings. And what constitutes a 'concrete situation and problem'? What would happen to a child who chose to study a concrete problem that led him to possible criticisms of the socialist-Zionist position? The possibility of such a thing happening is, of course, remote; for such undertakings would hardly be in line with the rule of the slowest member; and as all the themes have a distinctly Zionist flavour about them, no child presumably has ever been introduced to the possibility of such an idea. But in any case, immediate situations can never be detached from the ends which they subserve. Thus Mr. Ford's dichotomy between concrete situations and 'ends pursued for their own sake' seems to me to be confused. For the life of a socialist-Zionist, which the concrete situations chosen are intended to encourage, is an end pursued for its own sake; it is not a way of life that is in any way 'natural' to the children, but one that needs to be fostered consciously and with the greatest care. 'At Mishmar Haemek there was a calculated, but not a crude, attempt to foster certain very excellent human qualities and discourage others, and apparently it succeeded.' A possibility of assessing what Mr. Ford would regard as 'solid everyday achievement' is perhaps provided by an aside on the Settlement cobbler. This man, Mr. Ford asserts with obvious approval of the change—otherwise there would be little point in introducing the remark—once had a university job, I take it as a lecturer. Now I do not know the person concerned, and there may well have been good reasons for the change, of which I know nothing. But certain questions do raise themselves. At least the problem is posed as to whether the achievement of boots and shoes made is the best contribution that a man with the capacity to lecture in a university can make to mankind. Most people would agree that when Tolstoy gave up the pursuit of literature for a restricted social existence, he was not serving mankind in the manner to which he was best fitted. Many indeed can cobble; few can lecture. And Mr. Ford's approval seems to me to provide a further indication of the willingness to accept more immediate social usefulness, at the expense of less tangible but none the less real further ends, a habit which our age is all too frequently willing to adopt. In any case, there still remains the man's responsibility to himself. To escape from the world to become a cobbler may well be a subtle though none the less real way of evading responsibilities which are much greater where university teachers are concerned than for cobblers. The ethical implications of the parable of the talents at least deserves some consideration.

For in what does the boasted 'large measure' of freedom at Mishmar Haemek consist? The children are not 'free' to become anything but settlers; they are not 'free' to learn at a rate beyond that of the slowest; they are not 'free' to pursue any but a very limited range of topics with a distinctly propagandist flavour. Such restraints are indeed inevitable on those who choose or have chosen for them, specific and limited social ends. For as the social is only one aspect of man, the child is in fact being confined to what amounts to a very limited range of human possibilities, and can become 'free' only within those very restricting limits. We therefore arrive at the interesting but paradoxical situation that whereas Mr. Ford seemed to regard himself as the upholder of freedom against me, it was really I who stood for the larger freedom. For whatever else 'culture'[1] may be (in which I had in my article proclaimed myself a believer), it is the product and involves the experience of individual minds which, though aware of social relationships and their importance for man, are also aware of certain autonomies of the individual, and in many cases, of possibilities that go beyond both the individual and the social spheres. Culture therefore involves at least a consideration of something beyond the purely social; and the pursuit of culture *liberates* the human

---

[1] I use the word in a more self-conscious sense than does Mr. Eliot; I mean to refer to those valuable aspects of other men's minds, records of which have been left in various media, and an understanding of which is transmissible through conscious educational processes.

mind in a manner which the pursuit of a specific social end would not make possible. Why Mr. Ford should regard such a reversion to a more primitive, almost tribal structure, which he describes as the pattern of existence at Mishmar Haemek, as a significant human advance, I am unable to discover. And indeed, I suspect all such present day attempts at social integration. For true social integration can only be the by-product of the pursuit of some end which is not itself. To make social integration consciously the aim of human endeavour is to make something which is essentially human and imperfect—liable, that is to say, to the inadequacies of the planners of social integration —the standard, and thus to introduce immediately the possibilities of those disintegrative factors which criticism—to which the plan must, by its specifically human nature, for ever be open —of the schemes would involve. Hence the appearance of the concentration camp in those societies which have made man-made social plans the basis of their desire for social integration. For only thus can such criticism be suppressed, and the plan go forward.

A word of warning must end this. These criticisms, especially those of Professor Mannheim's ideas, must not be taken as arguments against all forms of popularization; provided the popularizer is completely aware of what he is doing he performs a very useful function. One would have imagined that the work of the late Susan Stebbing[1] and Mr. J. L. Russell[2] would have provided sufficient warning against a particular type of popularization which Professor Mannheim's views would seem to foster. Yet it is obvious, of course, that simplification—for the student in the textbook, for instance—is essential; certain simplified features of any subject must be grasped before it can be appreciated in its full complexity. But it must always be understood that what is being presented is not some quintessential knowledge that obviates the necessity of hard work and un-

[1] *Philosophy and the Physicists*, by L. Susan Stebbing, an analysis of the popular philosophy of Jeans and Eddington.
[2] 'The Scientific Best-seller', by J. L. Russell, printed in *Determinations*, edited by F. R. Leavis.

remitting labour later, but a different set of ideas that bears a relationship of varying degrees of crudity to the original. Provided that is realized, the popularizer performs a useful and desirable function in society. I have merely been concerned here to combat the idea, flattering to the common man, but vicious in its implications for our society, that what the popularizer can present is as good as—indeed almost preferable to—what can only be grasped by mature intelligences and complex minds. It would be a grave disservice to mankind and to those values that mankind has, at great pain and sacrifice, gradually evolved, to suggest anything different. There is, it seems to me, no escape from the problem of 'minority' values and the needful acceptance, by the common man, of the authority inherent in them. All men necessarily rest in incompleteness; it is in the nature of life that some must be more incomplete than others.

That Professor Mannheim's educational theories, implemented in the sort of school that Mishmar Haemek seems to be, contain many dangers, that the specific artistic judgements he passes reveal a blindness to true standards, will, I hope, be admitted. It is now necessary (to pass on) to consider what safeguards current theory provides for individual 'freedom' in education, and how adequate they are.[1]

[1] Perhaps the main effective historical source of the modern 'social' view of education has been the work of John Dewey, whose educational ideas have been based on the assumption that "what one is as a person is what one is as associated with others." (Cf. p. 94 below.) I have analysed the effects of Dewey's 'socialisation' of education and its repercussions on our present-day educational concerns in an article which will have appeared in the *Cambridge Journal* by the time this book is published; this article will, I trust, further validate the scattered criticisms of Dewey I make in this book. The essay is intended as part of a later work describing the historical rise of the 'progressive' movement. Mannheim is significant as a more nearly contemporary manifestion of the social, almost 'collectivist' attitude to education, and is, at this juncture, the more relevant figure.

CHAPTER THREE

FREEDOM IN EDUCATION

*'These charitable people never know vinegar from wine till
they have swallowed it and got the colic.'*
—GEORGE ELIOT: *Middlemarch*

It is characteristic of our present incoherence that at a time
when so much stress is being laid on the necessary submission of the individual to the needs of the social order (as
those needs are interpreted, all too frequently, in relationship to specifically material ends), a persistently influential
though not novel aspect of current educational theory should
be based on uncritical assertive claims for the individual. What
will be endangered by this, one suspects, is not so much the
immediate economic need of society as standards both of intellectual and emotional life, necessary preconditions to maturity. I have tried to show that 'order', as Professor Mannheim
conceives it, is mechanically and inadequately related to the
needs of human beings; I hope to show that some of the forces
making for 'freedom' and 'self-expression' are similarly tenden-
tious. For of both it is relevant to ask 'within what limits and
sanctioned by what *qualitative* consideration of the nature of
human life?' And in both cases the answers seem to me unsatis-
factory and culturally dangerous. For indeed it is not sufficient
merely to express what, on the surface, seem to be unexception-
able statements. It is not everyone who cries 'Lord, Lord' who
shall enter the kingdom of heaven; and the proffering of 'freedom' is not necessarily in itself desirable if the *quality* of that
freedom is not acceptable to a reasonably exacting standard.

At first sight the current agitation about education would appear reassuring; there would seem to be, as apologists would assert, a refreshing desire to experiment, to try new wine and to discard old bottles. But even the most strenuous enthusiast for the new ways cannot, if he pauses to think, find the pother completely reassuring. Change, as we have seen, is no end in itself; it normally betokens a lack of being—sound and fury have a habit of signifying nothing. The emphasis on experiment, one comes to suspect, conceals a basic uncertainty (a view reinforced by current insistence on method), an unconscious attempt to cover insufficiency by surface agitation. The whole uncertainty seems to spring ultimately from an inability to assess what constitutes an educated man; and that incapacity is in itself related to the uncertainty about the nature of man due to the abandonment of the theocentric solution to the problem, and the inability to construct a widely accepted and coherent anthropological substitute.[1]

Just as disconcerting are the implicit, sometimes explicit, claims made for education; it has come to be regarded as a panacea for our ills. Such claims reflect further that process, before referred to, by which responsibility is being shifted. It is always the next generation which is to pull the chestnuts out of the fire ('we look to youth . . .', words in the mouth of every prating politician); all that is needed is the necessary educational opportunity. This emphasis on education is related to the stressing of youth and the general adoption of the standards of youth—other disquieting symptoms. Only a civilization in decline, wishing to surrender that which constitutes civilization, could wish to avoid its responsibilities by projecting its hopes on to a future generation—jam to-morrow, as it were.

Indeed, this reverence for youth and the characteristics of youth, which are, of course, emotional rather than rational, deserves more careful analysis than it has received.[2] Part of youth's attraction lies in the fact that it is easier to see, and

[1] Cf. Ernst Cassirer: *An Essay on Man.*

[2] 'Children, fools, blackguards make of their inferiority a title for governing the world.'—Amiel.

55

therefore evade, the difficulties of rational behaviour than it is to realize even the need for standards of emotional behaviour. Feeling, to the immature mind, demands merely the exuberance of excess, as it did to the young Keats, for instance. Other ideas, however, are involved in the cult of youth. The decline in the belief in original sin and the corresponding affirmation of the natural goodness of man—all faults are the responsibility of 'the prison house'—both help to form it. A turning against the discipline inherent in full adult social living has, of course, been related to the rise to power of different social classes; and in the nineteenth century many of the more sensitive minds reacted against society because of the admitted barbarities of the social scene.

Many other causes could be discovered; but behind all the more immediate ones there is a whole tradition, based partly on immemorial pastoral convention and partly on a sentimentalizing of the Christian concern for the sanctity of the weak and lowly. This tradition has for long implied a background of criticism to the hard-won values of 'civilized' existence. In Shakespeare's day, nurture triumphed over nature, court over country as, for example, *The Tempest*, makes clear. But in our Faustian civilization there has always existed a yearning, often disguised under various social forms, but sometimes more obviously exposed, for a simple life (revealed, for instance, in the pastoral convention, or in our own day, in the intellectuals' neo-marxist cult of the working classes). This cult of simplicity helps to permit a release from the complexity of civilization and of the guilt that the conflicts of complexity engender. Such an attitude has not been allowed to develop fully during the sophisticated periods because of the protection provided by a sense of irony, which does not ignore such manifestations but only accepts them in relation to other modes of conduct. The seventeenth-century poet could write: 'Society is all but rude To this delicious solitude', and remain aware at once of the truth and falsity of the remark; but Wordsworth's feeling for Tintern Abbey is unequivocal. The eighteenth-century represents a moment of equilibrium in the breakdown of this irony:

56

yet even then the feeling for the unadorned and plain, the oft-repeated, the basic statement ('What oft was said . . .') contains the incipient suggestion of the simplifications of a later period. Baroque with its conscious superimpositions on the classic statement represents the last protest of an adornment which is not merely escapist. It may even be that the simplifications of geometrical order (e.g. the town plan, the formal garden) begin the process of levelling out which unconsciously degenerates into levelling down.

When, indeed, the possibilities of irony disappear because of the inability of the mind to stand aside from conflict, to detach itself—the detachment of irony is a feature of a degree of maturity, rarely of youth, and those who accept the valuations of youth must sacrifice it—when, in fact, the situation is felt to be 'serious' and the onlooker willy-nilly involved, partly because of a realization of personal instability and partly because the values of social living have broken down and failed to provide the necessary balance, then indeed there is a surrender to the mere sequence of events; 'being' is forced to give place to 'becoming'.[1]

What is obviously in process of becoming—youth—is sought after because its assurance of change represents paradoxically the only permanent value the mind can conceive. One aspect of nineteenth-century 'thought' unconsciously assumed such a surrender to the process of 'becoming'. To-day, in terms of numbers, which socially is all that seems to matter, it has become the predominant assumption. The effect of this cult of youth on the instability of intellectual and cultural interests with its consequent introduction of the exigencies of fashion into

---

[1] 'High seriousness', as nineteenth-century poetry and critical doctrine made clear, precludes in its single-mindedness an appreciation of its opposite; cf. the remarks about the '*fun*' of the people made by Matthew Arnold and quoted in Chapter Four. Arnold, in his *single* mindedness, and despite his intelligence, is a portent of what is to come. Relief is found in that which is obviously not 'serious' (in the nineteenth-century sense of the word), i.e. nonsense. This, in Carroll and Lear, etc., relates itself to the child in a manner which it would be interesting to pursue (cf. W. Empson, *Some Versions of Pastoral*).

the world of ideas is worth remarking upon. L. T. Hobhouse provides an interesting comment on the rapid change of dominant interests among the young with its encouragement of superficiality:

'These generations are extraordinarily short-lived. I can count up the intellectual fashions that have taken and held my students for a brief space. When I began in 1907 there was a wave of social idealism. Then very soon came suffrage, then syndicalism, then the war, then guild socialism, then Freud. . . . Each of these waves absolutely submerges everything for the time being; be the subject what it will, the students will always get it back one way or another to the popular topic. It's lost labour to refute these things—they just die out in time.'[1]

Such fashions, however, reach beyond the student world.

Now it is characteristic of the educational theory I am setting out to examine that it should apply to the education of youth those very mental habits that youth most assuredly displays. One conceives of education as at once a vitalizing *and a stabilizing* process, as an encouragement, not only of what its object already superabundantly possesses, but of other aspects that can only be attained by a *growing into*. Any mature theory of education should surely involve an appreciation of both factors in the irony of existence so that there shall be the possibility of coalescence and fusion which will help create the pattern of life. Certainly it must provide an element of 'being' in what can else only be a meaningless 'becoming'. Yet this is precisely what this particular educational theory I am setting out to examine does not profess—or glosses over in the light of other interests. Practice may do something to correct the imbalance of precept; but the characteristic stresses in such educational writings, as we shall see, betray an overall impression that must convey itself to the practitioner.

Roughly speaking—to sum up the movement, as it were— the changes have involved a shift of emphasis in our educational concerns. In all teaching situations there are three elements—

[1] *L. T. Hobhouse* by Hobson and Ginsberg, quotation from a letter.

the teacher, the subject matter of the instruction and the taught. In recent years the focus of attention has been on the last of these three terms, the taught, the children, in fact.[1]

The characteristic attitude of the 'new approach' is summed up in the words of a recent book on *Activity in the Primary School*: 'Our attention is focused, not on a system of education for children, but on the children themselves.' A recent pronouncement in *The Times Educational Supplement* stated that 'Few people nowadays are likely to challenge the view that the curriculum is made for the child, not the child for the curriculum.' And, for further corroboration, there are the words of the late and much-esteemed Susan Isaacs: 'The children themselves are the living end and aim of our teaching.' The three A's replace the three R's.

It need perhaps hardly be stated that the theories I am concerned with are offshoots of the Rousseau–Froebel–Pestalozzi line of educational thought—a line whose contribution can be summed up in the proposition 'a child's education ought to permit its freedom of development in accordance with the laws of its own nature'. Indeed, though I refer to these ideas as 'new' and 'progressive', it is a commonplace that many of them are in origin well over a hundred and fifty years old. Certainly most are inherent in the work of Froebel. They are essentially romantic ideas. They push the notion of the 'creativity' (a key word) of the individual mind to its uttermost limits so that development is seen as the result of the spontaneous activity of

[1] It may be argued that what I am about to say is partly invalidated because I am not sufficiently specific about the age of children involved. I am, however, concerned to combat a deliberate trend in educational policy that is spreading to the treatment of all ages. Naturally the extent of 'determination' on the part of the teacher will vary in accordance with age of pupil; psychological investigation would seem to show that the *degree* of control and of effort demanded where infants are concerned should differ from that expected of older children. But in all cases, as will emerge, I believe that education should be primarily deterministic, i.e. that it should be much more in the hands of the teacher to determine the nature of what is learnt, and that there should be a much stricter interplay between the child's interests and needs of the moment and the overall necessity of producing as mature an adult as innate mental capacity will permit, than present theory would encourage.

the inner being rather than of the formative power exercised by any outside authority. The child is to grow, not to be moulded (analogies drawn from natural life were frequent in Froebel). Hence the exercise of outside authority, in whatever form, is to be reduced to an absolute minimum.

Froebel was so convinced of the essential rightness of unimpeded inner development that he could write:

'We must presuppose that the still young human being, even though as yet unconsciously, like a product of Nature, precisely and surely wills that which is best for himself, and moreover, in a form quite suitable to him, and which he feels within himself the disposition, power and means to represent. . . . Men, who wander through your fields, gardens and groves, why do you not open your minds to receive what Nature, in dumb speech, teaches you?'

Such analogies drawn from nature are, of course, highly dangerous; for into man's development enters a self-consciousness that is entirely absent from the growth of natural things.

Yet, in replacing the mechanical conception of the mind by the biological, Froebel performed a great service to education. At the same time, the logical inconsistencies of his approach have been so admirably exposed by Mr. Charles D. Hardie in his *Truth and Fallacy in Educational Theory* that I prefer to recommend this book to the reader and consider instead some of the over-emphases inherent in the ramifications of the theory, and its cultural implications, points not touched upon by Mr. Hardie.[1] For in practice, such a philosophy lends itself to a decline of attainment and an overvaluation of certain qualities important within certain limits of control but dangerous when allowed unrestricted play.

It would be stupid, of course, to contend that what has developed from Froebel's theories constituted nothing but loss. There was a situation to be tackled—the situation George

[1] Cf. Chapter I of Mr. Hardie's book. Cf. too, on the whole problem of 'progressive' education, I. B. Kandel's *The Cult of Uncertainty*, and some cogent remarks in Dr. Eric James's admirable *Essay on the Content of Education.*

Bourne described in the quotation I gave in the first chapter. In the process of attempting to tackle it, as I have said, considerable good resulted. For one thing education—what goes on in the schools—has been brought more into line with real life—what goes on outside school. The attention which has been focused on the child has led us to consider and to assess much more carefully than heretofore the needs of the child—and the needs of the child in relationship to the particular environment from which the child has sprung. We know much more than we did about the nature of childhood and we have more reasonable educational expectations for our children of various ages, aptitudes and abilities. The teaching of the abstract and totally unrelated fact—in the manner for instance, advocated by Mr. Gradgrind in Dickens's *Hard Times*—the habit of memorizing by rote information quite remote from the child's possible range of experience, has gone, I trust for ever. There has arisen, perhaps, a too great contempt for facts as such—merely because they are facts, that is to say, regardless of their possible relevance or usefulness; but criticism of this sort must be made later.

As a result of this closer relationship between education and life, the child has had a more active and individual role assigned to him. Our investigations into the nature and make-up of the child have shown the need for the active participation of the child in the learning process. The mind is no longer regarded as a piece of blank paper, on which it is the function of the teacher to stamp what images he or she will; it is regarded as something active not passive, a real and not a sleeping partner in the learning situation. The child, too, has had much more attention paid to him as an individual; especially has this been so in the case of mediocre or backward children. The study of the emotional factors in education have shown us that backwardness is not necessarily a symptom of naughtiness or waywardness (though I do not think that such possible symptoms of childish egotism should always be ruled out).

The final outcome of all this, of course, has been to make the schools happier places than they have been. There is a better standard of relationship between teacher and taught than before. No longer, for instance, is it possible for the modern teacher to flog his pupil with quite the uninhibited vigour that seems not infrequently to have marked the habits of the Victorian pedagogue. We have all become far too self-conscious about our position and aims; we are infinitely more aware of the subtleties of the teaching situation than we were—perhaps over-aware.

Yet even if it were desirable—and I am not saying for one moment that it is—to cancel all that has occurred as a result of our new approach to teaching problems, it would be quite impossible to do so. If all revolutions occur in answer to some need, that does not mean that all which thus occurs is necessarily good. Yet it is no use trying to efface the notion of the revolution itself. These new teaching ideas have entered into our daily life and our consciousness and they must be accepted as having done so. History never repeats itself. We can never really go back to *status quo ante*.

But that does not mean that our acceptance need be uncritical. The process in the history of ideas tends to be dialectical —that is to say, the felt inadequacy of an idea leads to the statement of a new concept, which in the course of time coalesces with the older notion to form a synthesis. Our most important task in education to-day is to be thus synthetical. How much of the new, when we see it against a background of the traditional modes and purposes of the whole range of English educational practices, can we accept?

There is a certain ambiguity in the sentence I quoted above from *The Times Educational Supplement*: '. . . the curriculum is made for the child, not the child for the curriculum.' Neither, in a sense, is *made* for the other; but both exist; and in some sort of way, they must be made to come into relationship, a relationship not to be effected always at the expense of the curriculum. It is, after all, what a child learns that gives him significance— for without 'learning' of some sort, the child would be a mere living entity no more meaningful than the protoplasm. For, indeed, it should be obvious enough that the end of education is not the child, but the child transformed in accordance with a careful consideration of the relative stress to be laid on immediate ends and ultimate good. It is the latter, one feels, that is coming to be increasingly neglected, partly because of the mental limitations of a number of the teachers, partly because of the theory by which they are hindered and which fails to provide them with any precise conception of those ends.

I hope it will be clear that what I look for is not the *rigid* imposition of a set standard. George Eliot in *The Mill on the Floss* has some hard and adequate things to say about square pegs in round holes where the education of Tom Tulliver is concerned. But I want to re-kindle interest in the educational weft that is to combine with the warp of the growing mind to form the finished pattern. My concern, I would like to think, is related to that of Mr. T. S. Eliot in his diagnosis of the relation of the individual work of art and tradition:

'The existing order is complete before the new work arrives; for order to persist after the supervention of novelty, the whole existing order must be, if ever so slightly, altered; and so the relations, proportions, values of each work of art towards the whole are readjusted; and this is the conformity between the old and the new.'[1]

Both child and material must undergo a process of mutual adaptation, analogous to that suggested by Mr. Eliot between the historical works of artistic creation and the new work which will grow out of the old and yet retain its own individuality.

As, moreover, it will become obvious that what I have at the back of my mind in making this critique of current assumptions is a reassertion, among other things, of an older *tradition* of education (the tradition of learning, the 'authority' of human knowledge), I feel I must also, at the outset, signify my acceptance of Mr. Eliot's dictum: 'Tradition cannot mean standing still.'[2]

It might be well to begin by considering the current emphasis

[1] *Tradition and the Individual Talent.*
[2] T. S. Eliot: *After Strange Gods.*

on enjoyment and play methods. It has already been pointed out that the schools have become much happier places than they were. I hope I shall not be accused of wishing to increase the sum of human misery if I introduce a note of query here. Not very long ago, a primary school headmaster said to me: 'Of course, I don't very much mind what the children do here, provided they are happy.' I wonder about the wisdom of such a statement. I wonder still more about the idea of happiness being the *conscious* aim of any school. It is not that children shouldn't be happy; it is whether happiness as a specific aim is ever successful. Happiness comes as a by-product of the achievement of some end not itself, and the more we consciously wish to be happy, the more it eludes us. Moreover, very often, one is met with situations where present happiness must be sacrificed so that a future greater happiness can be achieved; there are in fact certain types of happiness that can only be achieved by the opposing and overcoming of immediate impulses and desires. This is a matter often for nice discrimination. But our purpose is to produce happy adults rather than happy children. Here it will be interposed that if the children are happy, then the adults will be happy too. Experience, however, does not always bear this out. The whole problem is confused, of course, by the inability to arrive at a proper definition of happiness; the pig in its sty usually looks contented, but the type of happiness it enjoys is not that proper to a human being. In that lengthy period of growing up, which, because of the subtlety of his mental equipment, man has to undergo, it is often necessary to perform tasks that are at the moment distasteful so as to acquire skills which can lead to profound happiness in later life. One of the great faults of 'child-centred' education has been its tendency to make the child its own arbiter in its own destinies. This situation has bedevilled in many ways the desirable introduction of play methods into schools. Play methods have been a valuable addition to our techniques, especially at an early stage. But 'play' in school should be purposeful in a way in which 'play' out of school need not necessarily be (except, perhaps, in the therapeutic sense of 'working off').

Plato's approval of play methods is often quoted; but it is interesting to note that Plato's attitude was very different from that of some of our educationalists, a fact which they often ignore:

'It is the community standpoint, not the "natural bent" of childhood, which is the dominating factor. Education takes the play-tendencies of childhood and directs and constrains them until the growing child takes on the mould of the rational, co-operative self-determining citizen. . . . Their immature minds are to be directly conditioned, from the very first, to take on the dye of the community laws, so that this shall be indelible.'[1]

It is perhaps because the modern community is so different a thing from the Greek City-State that to-day one could hardly approve such a community-centred education (as I have shown in my analysis of Mishmar Haemek); at any rate, not without careful consideration of just what aspects of modern community life would be inculcated. What, however, is important to note is that Plato's use of play is purposeful—as indeed it should be and that such purpose exists outside the child.

Modern play methods as seen in many schools seem often to fall down because they involve little but aimless and 'subjective' attempts to stimulate 'interest', with little regard to the value of the interest involved. Directed play—the learning of tables by drill can be made into play quite easily by a vital teacher—is valuable, of course. Thus objections to play arise not from play in itself but from the fact that the ends play is intended to sub-serve are becoming increasingly neglected. This is so partly because of a lack of clarity of definition, partly because precept removes the civilizing influence (at least to be assumed) of the teacher to too great an extent, and partly because of a funda-mental inability to relate the idea of what constitutes an edu-cated person to the apparent need of the moment.[2]

[1] R. C. Lodge: *Plato's Theory of Education*, 1947.

[2] Graham Wallas, in a valuable criticism of Froebel reprinted in *Men and Ideas* (it appeared as long ago as 1901) quotes this interesting remark made by an intelligent small boy: 'When they play they don't really play, and when they work they don't really work.' I have heard many intelligent modern children complain of boredom in 'free activity' infant schools.

The same may be said of the concern for interest: a child, it is said, should be allowed to develop its own interests in accordance with its needs—I repeat the jargon of any modern educational textbook. But interest is largely the creation of circumstance; it is not a thing a child is born with; and it is up to the teacher to create, not interest undefined, but the right sort of interest to develop the ultimate good of the child—by performing a very delicate but definite and positive function in its life. The sorts of interest which one can hope that civilized people will develop are in no way 'natural' to the human being. The contradictions, of course, are inherent in the looseness of the vocabulary used and the ambiguity of the terms. Interest is no end in itself, as seems to be imagined; there exist standards of interest. Children are interested in their excretory functions but no teacher would encourage such; the objections are too obvious. It is when the nature of the interest is more disputable that problems of value must be considered—and such problems all too frequently do not appear even to be raised. Moreover, mature interests that the teacher can see the need of much more readily than the child—playing the piano, for instance— usually involve initial drudgery that may well have to be imposed on the young if their good is to be pursued. A restriction too may be necessary where harmful interests are involved— Plato's ideas on 'music' are relevant here. Such problems of restriction must indeed be faced—and our society, for a number of reasons related to the decline of the notion of absolute values, the disintegrative effects on the personality of the Freudian analysis, the political egalitarian tradition, is not facing them.

One of the prime virtues, according to its apologists, of this sort of education is that it is supposed to afford a much greater measure of freedom to a child—freedom that is said to be essential in the process of growing up in a democratic society. In any case, these new methods spring, as we have seen, from a theory of the nature of man which values the spontaneous rather than the premeditated, the impulse rather than the conscious action, the emotional rather than the ratiocinative. Yet freedom in relation to human activities is a highly ambiguous concept. Indeed, the only really 'free' person is the lunatic; and his freedom is often of such a nature as paradoxically to need absolute restraint. All the higher freedoms of the human being imply the initial restriction and discipline essential to the process of becoming 'free' to exercise the required skill. It is the undisciplined mind that, so far as human beings are concerned, is the 'unfree' mind. The implications of Donne's address to God:

> *Take me to you, imprison me, for I*
> *Except you enthrall me, never shall be free.*

deserve some consideration.

Moreover, to face young children with the continual necessity of choice, which is what in effect progressive theorists do, is to remove from children the sense of security which an imposed ritual can often afford immature minds. To have to perform set tasks at a set time creates with young children a background of security that is vital for their development. It is arguable that some of the difficulties inherent in our culture arise, even at an adult level, from the disintegrative aspects of too great a freedom of choice; to provide such freedom at too early an age can lead to even greater insecurity. In any case, such freedom is often illusory. I once watched a class of infants, brought up on free activity methods, attempting to make paper hats for a Christmas party. Theory, though not perhaps common sense, demanded that no previous instruction be given, or so I was informed by the expert in infant method who accompanied me. One child finally evolved a very inadequate copy (the fashionable way of expressing it would be a 'creation') of a crown he had previously seen. The rest merely copied him. The argument is that the child should be free to choose what sort of hat he wanted, and that in finding out for himself how to achieve his end, valuable educational experience would be gained. The latter notion, pushed to its logical conclusion, would demand the recreation by each generation of the whole of human experience; for if the teacher is not allowed to instruct in the making of hats, why should she be allowed to instruct in anything? Carefully supervised and directed inquiry can be a useful educational technique; the expectation that children somehow recreate from within themselves forms which it has taken many years to evolve seems to me both dangerous and time wasting. [1]

In any case, choice—freedom of action—is not natural to the child, as I have suggested. It can only result from a prior capacity to understand the implications of the possible courses of action. No child is free to choose by the light of nature alone. His capacity depends entirely upon the choices that have previously been made for him by other people to enable him to be free to choose anything. Thus no child is free to choose until he is already sufficiently disciplined to see the implications of his choice. And, in such prior disciplining it is our duty as educators to shield him from harmful impulses that may later militate against his freedom of choice. Thus to submit the mind

[1] When this paragraph was originally published in *The Times Educational Supplement*, the following cricitism was made in 'Comment in Brief':

'If children are set to create paper hats, as though none had been made before and no models existed, it does not seem fair to argue that this implies a wasteful contempt for accumulated human knowledge. Mock attempts to produce the atmosphere of discovery have their value. It is no more than what is done sometimes at another stage in education—setting young scientists to carry out again one of the famous experiments of the past.'

Now indeed, 'mock attempts to produce the atmosphere of discovery have their value'; but it is significant that the illustration that *The Times Educational Supplement* chooses to employ, that of setting young scientists to re-create famous experiments, provides an excellent example of a type, all too frequent in educational argument, of imperfect analogy. For there are at least two important differences in the situation as between young scientists conducting experiments and infants making paper hats. Young scientists already know sufficient about science to realize the conditions involved, the *type* of thing that is being done; they have a background of understanding about the sort of processes involved in scientific experiments—they are, in fact, skilled in the *mode*, of which the experiment is only a feature of a general, comprehended approach. Secondly, the range of necessary attention and skill is much more restricted where the young scientists are concerned, in relation to age and experience, than it would be in the case of infants, who approach the problem of making paper hats for the first time, completely without fore-knowledge or the security of a background of instruction in the general principles of paper hat-making. In any case, young scientists in schools are normally given preliminary instruction in the exact nature of the experiment and its intended conclusion. One shudders to think what might happen in a chemical laboratory if the young scientists were let loose as unskilled in scientific method as these infants were unskilled in paper hat-making.

to a continual deluge of what, even in our easy-going society, could be accepted as bad influences and thus to blunt his power of discrimination is not to free the child but to bind him. Hence the paradox that to free the child we must submit him to some form of rigour. The freest mind is the great mind; and greatness as George Santayana has said, has 'character and severity'. Even more to-day is this note of rigour, severity, call it what you will, necessary, when 'a multitude of causes, unknown to former times, are acting with a combined force to blunt the discriminating power of the mind, and, unfitting it for all voluntary exertion, to reduce it to a state of almost savage torpor'. The description is taken from Wordsworth; its relevance to our present discontents is manifest, at a time when the 'craving for extraordinary incident', for sensationalism has so increased.

If then, the standard is to be freedom, that freedom itself implies the initial restraint and discipline inherent in the process of becoming free to exercise the required skill. It would not be necessary to stress what indeed seems so evident were it not that the whole of our teaching practice, either when 'free activity' methods or more formal ones are adopted, suffers from a basic confusion. The advance on the knowledge of child psychology is important in so far as technique is concerned, but it can have no effect on the aims and ends of education, which like the ends of life, I believe, 'exist' as absolute objectives,[1] and to be intimately related one to the other. To make the individual interests of the child the end is to abrogate all possibility of cultural coherence and in addition to deny the child what is essential, a sense of what is to be achieved. It is not too much to say that it is the function of the school to leave a child with a sense of and a respect for what he does not know, in addition to a confidence about such skills as he has succeeded in acquiring.[2]

[1] For reasons, of course, which it would be outside the scope of this book to discuss, though my essay on Newman may, by implication, introduce certain clarifications.
[2] That it is necessary consciously to accept limited ends for limited mentalities raises another though related problem. The fact is, however, that in the theory I am attacking such ends are not regarded as limited; the possibility inherent in the child becomes the end in itself.

But before pursuing this topic further, it may be useful to examine more specifically a recent pronouncement related to the theory under review. It will provide further information about the nature of the existence sanctioned by this theory; and it will afford a further interesting insight, to those unacquainted with current writing on educational problems, into the loose terminology all too frequently employed.

The extract is from a periodical symptomatically entitled *The New Era*, and it is part of an article on 'Group activity in School', by the late Professor H. R. Hamley, Professor of Education at the University of London Institute of Education:[1]

'In an article published in 1918, W. H. Kilpatrick, the father of the Project Method, tells us that he "appropriated the word 'project' to designate the typical unit of the worthy life". This puts the emphasis in the right place. The project, whether isolated or functionally related to other projects . . . is an echo of life, of life that is rich and significant, of life that is really worth living. If that is so, the characteristics of the project are the characteristics of the life that is worth living. Among them are the following: *purpose, significance, interest, spontaneity,* and *social co-operation.* A full discussion of these terms would lead us rather too far from our present purpose. The only term that may need a word of explanation is "spontaneity". Now it is one of the characteristics of life that it is not fixed or determined, strictly ordered or predictable; on the contrary, it is spontaneous and free, full of variety and enticing uncertainty. Life is a becoming, an unfolding, a continuous creation and no one knows with certainty what it will become or what the unfolding will finally yield. Where there is life, we say, there is hope. The glory of the project, whether it be an individual or a social project, is its *spontaneity,* its responsiveness to the evolving situation. No one knows, not even the teacher, exactly how it will turn out; no one knows the answer, for in many cases there is not one; at all events it cannot be found in any answer-book. The project has no pre-arranged standard either of appreciation or of attainment.'

[1] When this essay was first written, Professor Hamley was still alive.

Now it might be argued that this, because of its vagueness, does not merit discussion; and indeed, it would not were it not for the position held by its author, and the fact that it represents so well an attitude of mind that is being frequently adopted by our schools and colleges. I am not here concerned with the project method adequately handled (though I think there are grave dangers inherent in any attempt to correlate knowledge in such a way at too early a stage),[1] but with a vapidity of expression that is all too typical. Professor Hamley's characteristics of what used to be known as the 'good life' are so incoherently jumbled as to imply anything or nothing. It is hard indeed to see what purpose is served by applying a similar set of substantives to an intellectual concept like a project and to the life of an individual. But Professor Hamley's definition of 'spontaneity' is welcome, for the word, usually unexplained, crops up a great deal in this type of writing. As a human characteristic, 'spontaneity' seems to have attached to itself a peculiar charm of its own. It is perhaps pressing its meaning too far to ask precisely what significance in isolation such a term can have for human beings at all. For, as Wordsworth realized, even the most 'spontaneous overflow of powerful feelings' is yet inextricably related to the prior necessity of long and deep thought that he quite rightly thought essential to the act of creation; such a period of gestation was inherent in the act. Correlations can be made in the mind which, leading to new fusions of thought, give an appearance of 'spontaneous' creativity (cf. Coleridge's views on Imagination). But all this assumes a prior discipline, a 'subservience strictly to external things'. There must, in Coleridge's own phrase, be a 'correlation of subject and object'. Such ideas, as far as one can judge, do not appear to be part of Professor Hamley's intention (although, indeed, that intention is so vaguely expressed that it is difficult to pin Professor Hamley down in any precise way). What, however, he seems to be concerned with is a lack of restraint, a venting of the impulse of the moment, the deliberately unpremeditated quality of what happens.

[1] Mr. Hardie summarizes some objections to the project method, op. cit., pp. 58-9.

Such ideas are very common in contemporary teaching of art; they form, indeed, the main staple of the theory. Vast claims are made for the teaching of the visual arts which seem to me to be invalid (though no one will accuse me, I hope, of under-rating the importance of the arts). Mr. Read, for instance, goes so far as to assert that 'the secret of our collective ills is to be traced to the suppression of the spontaneous creative ability in the individual'. Such claims seem to be bound up with an over-emphasis on certain qualities, such as imagination,[1] which need a much more thorough critical investigation than can be afforded here, but to the need for which I can at least draw attention. It is true, of course, that the child's vision is different from that of the adult; but that does not mean that any and every manifestation of the child's 'imagination' has an equal validity. Interference by the adult seeking a greater perfection within the range of the child's convention seems to me perfectly valid, and an essential element in the child's development and growing up. Thus, in a recent article on 'Arts and Crafts',[2] Mr. Green's assertion that 'the expressive and imaginative qualities of a drawing will always be more important than mere factual statement', seems a remark of doubtful validity, without a prior investigation into the *quality* of the imagination and expression involved.[3] And Mr. Green's uneasiness betrays itself when he discovers that there is 'no artistic lapse in making a precise drawing of a plant, showing careful research into its structure. . . . It was not beneath the dignity of masters of the stature of Dürer and many others to make such drawings.' It was not indeed, though such precision, of course, is beyond the capacity of very young children. The capacity of such realism

---

[1] 'Down with imagination in schools, down with self-expression.'—D. H. Lawrence: *Education of the People.* Cf. Chapter 6.

[2] Printed in *The Quality of Education*, ed. D. Thompson and James Reeve.

[3] Imagination, loosely used, too often comes to mean 'fantasy-life'. The stimulation of this quality is all too much encouraged as it is, in our civilization of the cinema and the 'tuppeny blood'. When, again, it is urged that the child is to be told to draw 'what he sees', the results all too frequently are the consequence of bad factual statement. The use of the word 'imagination' and especially that of 'creative' seem to me to merit the fullest investigation.

represents a certain stage of development, which it is the function of the art teacher to encourage at the right time. It should certainly not be neglected.

Many children possess a certain gift of expression and are capable of evolving naïve and simple patterns; but no achievement of any real worth is possible without a long and arduous submission to the need of acquiring a technique by means of which what in fact is observed of 'nature' can be adequately conveyed to the viewer. The proper time to introduce various techniques requires careful consideration, for the child's view does, as I have said, in many respects, undeniably, differ from the adult's; nevertheless, it is partly through increasing mastery of technique that a young adolescent is enabled to develop a truly adult and mature sensibility. For the acquiring of technique surely has a repercussion on what in fact the artist 'sees'; for, in this case, increased technical accomplishment *can* aid the student's imaginative grasp of his subject . . . if the student has the necessary artistic integrity and capacity.

It is odd indeed that the practice of art teachers in this respect would seem to fly in the face of the experience of all the great masters; and it is instructive to examine the practice of the one great artist, who has been quoted to exemplify the results of 'spontaneity', William Blake. Mr. Anthony Blunt has irrefutably shown how much Blake depended upon a careful study of the work of his predecessors. Blake's own words testify to what he thought about careful copying:

'. . . no one can ever Design till he has learned the Language of Art by making many Finished Copies both of Nature and Art and of whatever comes in his way from Earliest Childhood. The difference between a bad Artist and a Good One Is: the Bad Artist Seems to copy a Great deal. The Good one Really does Copy a Great deal,'

and a little later: 'Servile Copying is the Great Merit of Copying.'[1] Admittedly in his quarrel with Reynolds' views on art as

[1] Anthony Blunt: *Blake's Pictorial Imagination*, published in the Journal of the Warburg and Courtauld Institute (1943). Cf. too, Lawrence's remarks on copying in his essay, *Making Pictures*.

an imitation of nature based on the necessity of following 'the other masters as a guide on making the selection necessary to arrive at a general idea of nature', Blake gave vent to such remarks as: 'Imagination is My World: this World of Dross is beneath my Notice', and 'Knowledge of Ideal Beauty is Not to be Acquired. It is Born with us'; but these statements seem to have had largely a polemical value, the product of an emotional reaction against Reynolds's ideas. Blake's practice shows how carefully he followed the masters, as Mr. Blunt has conclusively shown; and his remarks on copying show that in his imaginative efforts he was conscious of depending on a prior discipline.

It is possible that some art teachers would argue that their aim is not to train artists, but that the worth of 'free expression' lies in a certain therapeutic value; it is regarded as a means of ridding the child of his inhibitions by giving him scope to exercise his creative faculties. Despite Mr. Herbert Read, however, it is difficult to see the final therapeutic value of the type of free expression permitted, if such 'free' expression is allowed to go on too long. For an essential part of any mental therapy lies surely in the re-ordering of experience in relationship to something other than itself, a coming to terms with that which lies outside the self, and the consequent emergence of the self on a new level of experience; this involves a submission at some stage to a discipline of a sort, a discipline for which the theory seems to make too little allowance. It is a pity that in their reaction against a bad technique—that which produced the stilted, naturalistic drawing of the last century—art teachers should have thrown over all efforts to impart technique and followed Professor Cizek's dictum: 'Each child is a law unto himself and should be allowed to develop his own technique.' Even more astonishing are the claims made for child art, claims which seem to betoken a surrender to a naïve and singularly restricted range of experience. Mr. R. R. Tomlinson, in *Children as Artists*, states that:

'No claim is made by the author that children's drawings have the same art content as the work of adult artists, but he

74

does contend that they have a similar appeal to the emotions.'

It is necessary to draw attention to the question-begging use of 'similar'.[1]

I suggest, then, that it would not be impertinent at least to hint a doubt—I wish to do no more, for the 'new' movement in art has undoubtedly produced stimulating results—and to suggest that a more astringent investigation into the nature of the theory relating to 'spontaneous expression' is called for. What Professor Hamley has further to say, about life as a 'becoming', etc., is so trite as to be hardly worth saying. It is true in the sense that no one knows precisely what the future holds. To make this obvious fact an excuse for the abeyance or the depreciation of attempts at rational forethought and control—qualities that go to distinguish what is specifically man—is to abandon an important element on which man has built up his civilization. The freedom Professor Hamley so ardently admires is, as I have suggested, partly the fruit of this forethought. To be at the mercy of the 'evolving situation' is to be bound by accident and temporary exigence—to become like Hamlet passion's slave and hence to lose the native hue of resolution. Though the restrictions of a narrowly rational approach will, as we have seen, preclude a complete assessment of the imponderables in a changing situation, a profounder rationalism will allow for this. Professor Ginsberg's realization that 'Reason may recognize the value of spontaneity' admits that the 'adjustment of the claims of this value to the needs of control is one of (reason's) most difficult tasks'; but the difficulty does not provide an excuse for failing to make the attempt. The happiness that lies beyond the reach of art is yet the product of that art. To assert that

[1] This admittedly short book, with its uncritical formulation of the current theory, lays itself open to attack on many occasions. There is, for instance, the remarkable statement that 'Primitives (of the school of Giotto and Cimabue) . . . resemble children in one essential respect; in their artistic urge to explore with zeal entirely new paths, untutored and unaided.' How many children, in fact, do explore 'entirely new paths'? And is the *exploration* of *new* paths in itself so desirable, or do we merely bemuse ourselves with an outworn romantic vocabulary?

'the project has no pre-arranged standard either of appreciation or attainment' is to ignore the aim which may be exceeded
but alone gives meaning to the undertaking.

Yet this new approach has received increasing official sanction. The much-quoted words of the ministry's report on *The
Primary School* are relevant. There it is stated that 'the curriculum is to be thought of in terms of activity and experience rather
than of knowledge to be acquired and facts to be stored'; and
such a thesis is being maintained in the years beyond the primary school. As a result of the contempt which is being increasingly directed against the 'bookish few', that 'activity', which is
so cardinal a feature of modern educational policy, is being
thought of more and more in purely physical terms. That physical movement is a necessary feature of the development of
children is an indisputable fact; it is the relative emphasis that
is becoming disquieting. 'Activity', indeed, has become one of
the key concepts among our modern educational notions. It is
often asserted that children 'need' activity; and because nowadays our educational ventures tend to be circumscribed by what
the psychologists can assess about the natures and needs of
children, 'active' methods of education are very much in vogue.
It is true that children need to participate actively in what is
going on. Blake's remark that the fool sees not the same tree as
the wise man meant that even the most common of objects
needed an actively participating mind for its apprehension.
Coleridge was expressing the same notion when he spoke of the
coalescence of subject and object, of mind and that which exists
outside the mind, as the true mode of apprehension. Cardinal
Newman was hinting at it when he analysed the difference
between what he called 'real' and 'notional' assents.

But there is the need for a genuine coalescence; and if it is
true that children need activity, which implies a giving out, it is
also true that they need receptivity, a taking in.[1] I remember a

---

[1] Cf. an interesting and all too tantalizingly brief little essay on '*Enlightened*' *Education* by Alan Keith-Lucas, which appeared in *Scrutiny*, September 1932. After referring to the philosophy of Lao Tze, Mr. Keith-Lucas
proceeds: 'The point in question is the "outward flowing" and "backward

headmistress, who had just, as it were, inherited a free activity school, complaining of the inability of the girls to listen to what was being said to them. After all, learning how to listen is an important educational undertaking. It is not true that busy arms and legs always mean busy minds. It cannot be over-emphasized that in schools our primary consideration is the training of *minds*; for activity—any activity—is quite futile and meaningless unless it is guided by a sense of purpose; and the comprehension of purpose belongs to the realm of the mind. Again, experience (by which is usually meant impressions received from the immediate physical environment) only ac-quires significance as it is related to knowledge—there is a correlation between the two and to emphasize the one at the expense of the other is to impoverish the meaning of experience itself. When Keats wrote that he did not think anything could be known for truth until it had been 'proved upon our pulses', he ignored the fact that the possibility of response to experience is not innate, and that prior knowledge, even of mere despised 'fact', may well enable the experience, when it is undergone, to take on meaning—or at least, a deeper meaning. Thus my ex-perience of certain of the difficulties of emotional growth will be deepened by a prior reading of, say, *Hamlet*. The assumption of the report is that knowledge cannot become 'real' until it has been directly verified, a view which, one would have thought, has been sufficiently exploded. For it involves the setting up of only one criterion of the 'real'—that of sensory experience.[1]

flowing" methods: the contention that too much creative action leaves the "soul" wasted, so that at death it becomes "kusi", a daemon or unsubstantial ghost.'

[1] It is interesting to note that the subject-matter of even grammar-school education has become increasingly pragmatic over the last hundred years. (In a sense, of course, it is true that most education has always had a prag-matic bias, for there was a time when a knowledge of Latin had a severe practical value. But the pragmatic has undoubtedly received more consider-able emphasis in recent years.) Partly this may have been inevitable; but the fact that we may be faced, for instance, with an almost complete aban-donment of classical education because such a training is not directly applicable to everyday experience and is not itself the fruit of the need of the moment is symptomatic. I am not, of course, concerned to argue the virtues or vices of a classical training. I am concerned with the objections

This over-emphasis on physical activity, encouraged by the practical, pragmatic philosophy of the day, and by this notion that what children learn must always necessarily be the result of their own direct immediate experience, has led to a serious depreciation of the value of a verbal and linguistic education. The emphasis on 'things not words' stretches back as far as Bacon and Hall and other seventeenth-century writers. Their opposition, of course, was to the sterile and verbal gymnastics of the scholastic philosophers. Only recently has the attack been turned against linguistic training in itself. A visit to the local tram sheds is nowadays regarded as an educationally desirable venture; the study of poetry, indeed any form of book study, seems to be regarded with increasing hostility. A considerable amount of animus, at the present moment, is directed against what is known as 'mere verbalism'. The illustration, made respectable under the name of 'visual aid' is rapidly taking the place of the printed word. Perhaps it is not regarded as very democratic to be more highly skilled in the use of words than one's fellows; those who are more fluent can be dismissed as the 'bookish few'. Our social consciences call us from the solitariness of reading to the group or communal activity of a visit to the local gas works. And yet no experience, whether it be of the tram sheds, health centres or local farm lands, takes on conscious significance, unless the capacity to express, verbally, the findings matches the potentialities of the experience. Language, the capacity of expression, is an essential pre-requisite to the assimilation of experience in any form that is capable of having a vital and meaningful significance for the individual. Correlations in the mind can only be made as the result of an awareness, in which linguistic capacity for expression plays a vital part, of possible relational significance.

Especially in the age of television and the strip cartoon does it seem important to stress the value of books and book learning. An enormous amount of our knowledge must inevitably be

which lie behind its unpopularity, and which would be equally applicable to any other discipline (e.g. a deeper study of English) which was put in its place.

second-hand, must, in fact be learnt through books; it is just not possible to achieve first-hand verification of all aspects of knowledge; and certain types of knowledge can only be arrived at through linguistic descriptions of them, whether by word of mouth, or through books. Emotional states of mind, for instance, can only be conveyed in any degree of subtlety through words; to the highest expressions of these states of mind we give the name of poetry. I am not concerned to decry the value of direct, first-hand experience; but I am concerned lest too great an anxiety for immediate experience, with its essential limitations of scope, should lead to a decrying of other valuable means to knowledge. It is not necessary to have murdered before we can realize what Macbeth felt. Our knowledge of books, indeed, can often enrich our first-hand experience by making us more aware of the possible implications of that experience; and it is our job in the schools to give children some capacity to discriminate between books, in however limited a way.

Another of the more deplorable effects of the current laxity, of course, lies in the increasing abdication of the function of the teacher already referred to in the first chapter. His or her job is becoming more and more that of merely providing an adequate environment so that the children shall be able 'to follow up lines of interest and exercise every muscle in their bodies and every faculty of their minds', as Miss M. V. Daniel exuberantly proclaims, with what appears to be insufficient realization of the full implications of what she is saying. This abdication seems to afford merely another aspect of the general abandonment of intellectual and moral leadership in our society. The whole unwillingness to provide a view of life means, in many cases, that a worse view will be adopted, for a child cannot live in a vacuum, and there is little in the environment of most children to which they can look for guidance. One would have thought that the need for demanding standards—or at least creating a framework, which, while permitting a certain flexibility, would rigidly exclude deleterious interests and pursuits—was never more necessary than to-day when the teacher is one of the few civilizing influences in our vulgarized social order.

Indeed, the whole tendency towards making the child his own standard in the name of initiative and self-confidence is to be condemned as corrupting to the child. Self-confidence, as those who have taught know, so frequently comes to mean a self-satisfaction based on the type of egotism George Santayana so strongly and rightly condemns:

'Egotism is always a vice because founded on a mistake. It assumes, if it does not assert, that the source of one's being and power lies in oneself . . . and that nothing should control the mind or the conscience except the mind or the conscience itself.'

There are indeed enough of the low on whom assurance sits leaving our schools without multiplying their numbers by intent. I have encountered an educationist who has advised students not to mark children's essays unless invited by the children to do so. Not long ago an article appeared by a former inspector, in which, on the subject of an early writing lesson, she asserted that there must be no question whatsoever of 'Try harder'. That such ideas are bandied about is symptomatic of an attitude of mind which places an entirely undesirable emphasis on the egotism of the child mind. For the child to feel that it has a claim to attention is one thing; to feel that that claim has always to be met is pervasively corrupting to those very virtues of initiative and self-reliance that the romantic educationists profess to encourage. Such egotism, indeed, involves, on the part of the child, the loss of a sense of obligation and of the conception of contract inherent in any undertaking. Hence, ultimately, self-respect, which is the offspring of renunciation much more than of self-indulgence and which is involved in the admission of obligation, suffers. There is a loss of the 'tension' between individual mind and intractable material which many of the greatest minds (Goethe is a case in point) have found to be a necessary pre-requisite to achievement.

As I have already indicated, this outlook is closely related to a vast change that is taking place in our social structure and the balance of political power. It is realized that, now that for the first time in human history a whole population is being educated, and thus clamours for attention, a vast majority can find no place in the traditional educational system, for their mental abilities are inadequate to the discipline exacted. It is argued that nevertheless the mediocre must have their chance; as the Harvard Committee report expresses it:

'The record of such people over history—the simple-hearted, those who have done the unobserved work of this world—is certainly at least as good as that of their more gifted—and more tempted—brethren. They are as worthy and as valuable democratic citizens as anyone else.'

The second sentence, of course, is not necessarily true, as it should hardly be necessary to insist; it accords ill, in any case, with the committee's recognition that some ideas are more valuable than others, for in some sense of the word, 'ideas' are obviously the 'products' of individual minds, and the progenitors of more valuable ideas are therefore, to some extent at least, of greater worth to the community. But in any case it should be sufficiently clear that no society can exist for long that allows itself to be governed by the values of the mediocre in the manner encouraged by our civilization. The problem of how to reconcile the standards of maturity with the requirements of the many—the central problem of 'mass civilization and minority culture'—is not, however, to be met by a chaotic throwing-over of such standards as still survive at the behest of the individual, regardless of the individual's capacity and right to be considered. Even if with sections of our population limited educational aims are necessary—and of course they are—the fact that they are so limited must be clearly recognized and explicitly allowed for. The aim for any one group must recognize the ambiguity inherent in the idea of 'need', and must also realize its place in the hierarchy; then the 'needs' can be related to what is also desirable and it can be seen that their gratification is controlled by an appreciation not only of the individual's felt requirement but of the highest truths known to man. Finally the standard implicit in the aim, however limited, must be exacted. A careful appreciation of the dignity inherent in even a limited undertaking—limitations consciously appreciated—would be preferable to a system that makes a superficial know-all of even the commonest of men.[1] It is for reasons of this sort that attempts to secure a 'general education' that will provide a 'common core of knowledge' which the Harvard Committee is concerned to obtain in America by emphasizing the necessity of a common syllabus based on the Humanities, the Sciences and Social Studies, need to be regarded with a certain degree of suspicion. How this syllabus is to be adapted to the needs of the less able is carefully glossed over; it is only stated that it is to involve '*new and authentic* treatments of these great subjects, not simply waterings-down of harder courses for the less able'.[2] All this is too reminiscent of Professor Mannheim's 'essentials' to need analysis here.

It should be clear that the educational theory I have been examining reaches far beyond the purview of the school and is at once a reflection of and a further means of implementing the profoundly anti-rational forces we have seen at work in our own day. By failing to distinguish adequately between the relative worth and stability of impulses and feelings, by making, in its extremest form, the individual's desires and attainments the final test, by encouraging the belief that possibilities of attainment are not subject to rational analysis where what is essentially irrational and incapable, the child, is concerned, this theory proclaims its adherence to a body of ideas that is and has been destroying the wisdom of the European tradition on which our civilization has been built. I need hardly perhaps point out its relevance to that outlook which regards taste, for instance, as

[1] One of the current dangers lies in the contemporary condemnation of specialization. One appreciates the danger of over-specialization; but if some critics had their way, very soon instead of a few knowing a good deal about something nobody would know very much about anything. Cross fertilization is important, but there has to be something to fertilize. Again, it is necessary to distinguish between different sorts of specialisms. Thus to specialize in English literature would produce a very different and much more harmonious personality, in the Greek use of the term, than would concentration on some minute aspect of scientific investigation.

[2] *General Education in a Free Society*, report of the Harvard Committee (1946). My italics.

something essentially relative, and the phrase 'I like it' as the first and last words in literary criticism.

This essay is to be regarded as complementary to my remarks on planning and popularization, the obverse side of the picture. I have tried to show that in neither the mechanical rigidities of Professor Mannheim, nor in the careless abandonment of our hard-won values at the behest of a sentimental concern for the more immediate interests and needs of the individual, whether child or adult, lies our true way. Though I believe, with Newman, Arnold and Lawrence, in their various ways, objective values to 'exist', our human imperfection does not enable us to grasp them completely, which means that an adequate outlook must always be prepared to admit the implications of new aspects of knowledge; these may necessitate a careful reassessment of certain values in the light of new experience. But the necessity of such 'spontaneous' knowledge must not prevent our acting in accordance with the highest values mankind has discovered in the necessity imposed on us of determining the conditions by which we are to live. An abandonment to the immediate interests of the moment, in the name of an illusory freedom, would be as disastrous as a submission to the strait-jacket of the economic planner's will—indeed both are much more closely related than at first sight would seem obvious. An educational outlook affects and is affected by the quality of the age of which it is a manifestation. The inadequacy and superficiality of many of our educational ideas is a sad comment—if comment there need be—on our inability to assess adequately the requirements either of freedom or of order.

Yet freedom and order—in education and in social life—are both essential; and the careful determination of their mutual claims is one of the age-long efforts of mankind. The notions of 'freedom' and 'order' we have examined so far have been based on too narrow conceptions of what is implied by 'freedom' or 'order'. In the case of the planners this is perhaps obvious enough; it is a little more difficult to see that modern educationalists, with their encouragement of 'spontaneity', are guilty of a similar degree of abstraction. Yet a little thought will show that it is so. For what, in the last resort they are doing, as the terms in which they express their conceptions make clear, is to take the abstract, political notion of 'freedom' which they derive from their democratic assumptions and apply it to children.[1] We live in a society which values *a certain conception* of 'freedom' —roughly, 'freedom from' rather than 'freedom for'. When, therefore, we come to examine the 'needs' of children, we bring with us those mental and abstract assumptions about the nature of man which our society has taught us and we project this into our diagnosis. Thus the conception of 'freedom' which actuates our modern 'scientific educator' (as Matthew Arnold contemptuously referred to him—and with some show of reason) is a very different thing, as we shall see, from the conception of 'freedom' which lies behind the work of a writer like D. H. Lawrence, even though both tend to use a similar vocabulary.[2] We live in a profoundly materialistic age; it was Lawrence who pointed out how much our ideals—of freedom, for instance— are merely a manifestation of that materialism: 'An ideal established in control of the passional soul is no more and no less than a supreme machine-principle;' and thus he diagnoses that 'Ideal and material are identical. The ideal is but the god in the machine—the little, fixed, machine principle which works the human psyche automatically.'

Part of our difficulty lies in the fact that our conceptions of 'freedom' and 'order' exist only in individual or narrowly social terms. The thesis I wish to maintain is that they can only be adequately conceived in terms of something which transcends the individual and the social spheres. We need, in fact, to meet on that 'third ground', that 'holy ground' to which Lawrence refers. What I mean by this will, I hope, become plainer when I examine the ideas of two great educators—one representative of 'order' at its highest, the other of 'freedom'—writers whose understanding of human nature is profound and whose educa-

---

[1] Thus I know of university lecturers in education whose concern that the child or student shall be 'free' is as rigid and basically as tyrannous as any rigid disciplinarian of the old school.

[2] Cf. pp. 162 seff.

tional ideas are correspondingly enriched, writers, too, who take into account aspects of human personality which are almost totally neglected to-day. At least they will afford a release from that modern hell which, after Sartre, might not undeservedly be described as 'oneself and other people'; as Berdyaev has expressed it: 'Man ceases to know himself when he knows of no higher being or principles than those contained in the confined circle of his own nature.' There, indeed, we have it; and we have just examined two manifestations of what appears to me to be man's inability to know himself.

But before we plunge into Newman and Lawrence, the two educators I have in mind, let us examine one of the best of the humanist positions, that of Matthew Arnold. Though Arnold's outlook is not actively religious, it is concerned with recommending something in terms of which individual and social man can transcend himself—culture. And religious values need to be informed by the spirit of culture at its best, as Newman himself saw.

CHAPTER FOUR

MATTHEW ARNOLD, H.M.I.

*'Every one shuts himself up in his own breast, and affects
from the point to judge that world.'*
—ALEXIS DE TOCQUEVILLE: *Democracy in America*

T he importance of Matthew Arnold as an educationalist—the reason why, to-day, we should do well to
turn to him for light—seems to me to lie in at least
two directions. There is his diagnosis of a particular
cultural situation, a situation which since Arnold's day has not
only grown worse, but has grown worse along the lines that
Arnold indicated; and there is his appreciation of the necessity
of tackling the current degeneration of standards by a clear-
sighted understanding of the essential distinctions to be made
between means and ends in education—a capacity which arises
from his ability to conceive them in a wider context.

Arnold was appointed to the inspectorate in 1851. He had
sought the appointment because he desired to get married; and
he was in fact married during that year. He pursued his work
until his resignation in 1886, becoming Senior Inspector in 1870
and Chief Inspector in 1884. He made several trips to the Con-
tinent to gain information about educational systems abroad,
reporting at various times on the systems of France, Germany,
Switzerland and Holland. He can thus be regarded as a pioneer
in comparative education.

The inspectorate was, then, a means to an end for him,
rather than an end in itself. Although he became extremely
interested in the wider issues of educational policy, and prob-

ably exercised, through his brother-in-law, W. E. Forster, a certain influence on parliamentary policy, the day to day routine of inspection did not much appeal to him. Towards the end of his career, when he was thinking of retiring, he expressed the hope that he would not perform 'the dance of death in an elementary school'. His early letters are full of complaints:

'I have had a hard day. Thirty pupil teachers to examine in an inconvenient room, and nothing to eat except a biscuit, which a charitable lady gave me.'

A little later:

'I got here a little before two, had a sandwich, and then went to the school. I don't know why, but I certainly find inspecting peculiarly oppressive just now; but I must tackle to, as it would not do to let this feeling get too strong.'

To his wife, he wrote:

'I am too utterly tired out to write. It certainly was nicer when you came with me, tho' so dreadfully expensive; but it was the only thing that could make this life anything but positive purgatory.'

At the same time, he realized the importance of the schools:

'. . . their effects on the children are so immense, and their future effects in civilizing the next generation of the lower classes, who, as things are going, will have most of the political power of the country in their hands, may be so important.'

Arnold's diagnosis of the cultural illness of his society he gives at length in *Culture and Anarchy*. It is perhaps too well known to need a detailed account; but some reference must be made, because his social criticism lies behind his work as an inspector, informing it, though, oddly enough, as we shall see, not receiving the material witness from his knowledge of schools one might have expected.

Briefly, his indictment of his age amounts to a condemnation of the materialistic and mechanistic spirit that pervaded mid-

Victorian England. He answers the charge of 'selfish ease and indecision in action' that Frederic Harrison made against the men of culture by pointing out the need for those qualitative considerations in social life which only cultivated minds were capable of making. Far from being a luxury, the man of culture was an essential refining element among the coarse and ill-considered movements of the day. Culture, then, has an important social function to perform, a function that 'is particularly important in our modern world, of which the whole civilization is, to a much greater degree than the civilization of Greece and Rome, mechanical and external, and tends constantly to become more so. But above all in our own country has culture a weighty part to perform, because here that mechanical character, which civilization tends to take everywhere, is shown in the most eminent degree.'

He points out that most of the ends which the mid-Victorians so acclaimed were but 'machinery', means to further ends—even 'freedom' was only machinery.

The man of culture, then, was a vital member of society; he not only sought 'perfection', he aimed to make it prevail, in opposition to action for the sake of action: of this we shall say more later. Culture he defined as the 'pursuit of our total perfection by means of getting to know, on all matters which most concern us, the best which has been thought and said in the world; and through this knowledge, turning a stream of fresh and free thought upon our stock notions and habits, which we now follow staunchly but mechanically, vainly imagining that there is a virtue in following them staunchly which makes up for the mischief in following them mechanically.'

(Such a definition appears, of course, to be highly abstract. What validates it are the particular judgements which he makes in the body of his criticism and which, by implication, illumine his conception—judgements which make Arnold the best of nineteenth-century critics.[1]) The current trouble was, he diag-

[1] So that if we are asked what Arnold meant by 'culture', we can point to his criticism as providing a body of concrete evidence of his capability to implement the general remarks in *Culture and Anarchy* by a series of individual

nosed, the English like 'to be doing something and doing it as (they) please, and (do) not like the trouble of thinking and the severe constraint of any kind of rule'. Hence some check on the unrestrained liberalism of the time was necessary. Arnold proclaimed himself a Liberal—but 'a Liberal tempered by experience, reflection and renouncement'. The renouncement to which he sought to persuade his fellow Victorians had two agencies: the state and some centre of enlightened opinion (such as an academy) that would serve to purify the tastes of the day. His conception of the state was perhaps a little naïve; the State, he thought, was made up of our 'best selves', and the action of the State was the action of our best selves, working together, as opposed to the operation of our 'ordinary selves' which functioned when we were split asunder, 'doing as we liked'. Modern history does not perhaps always bear out Arnold's notion of what happens when the State intervenes: but his idea of the State has some importance for his educational thinking. During the time that Arnold was Inspector, the whole question of the responsibility of the State for education was being thrashed out in Parliament. Between 1850 and 1870, no fewer than eighteen Education Acts were passed by Parliament, and fourteen Bills concerned with elementary education were presented to Parliament. Arnold, of course, was an enthusiastic supporter of State intervention in education; his experience in France and Germany pointed to his mind many of the advantages that would accrue to education as a result of the intervention of the State. There is a certain topical humour to be derived from one of his remarks: 'What influence may help us to prevent the English people from becoming, with the growth of democracy *Americanized*? I confess I am disposed to answer: Nothing but the influence of the State.'

At the moment, however, it is more important to consider the second check on unrestrained Liberalism that he proposed.

He saw clearly the cultural consequences of there being no

comments which, because of their intelligence and coherence, command our general respect; though certain weaknesses are also present as is pointed out below.

centre of enlightened opinion such as the French had in their Academy, that might at once set and correct the cultural standards of the age. Matthew Arnold's 'Culture' was, of course, a self-consciously acquired taste and appreciation which he thought contact with the 'best which has been thought and said in the world' would bring; at the same time, it involved a protest against the romantic idea that the source of enlightenment lay within the self. It implied the reassertion of a classical ideal and involved a submission to an external discipline, a discipline that was regarded as something creative and refining, not stultifying and deadening. For, indeed, Arnold realized that genuine creativity was the product of a co-operation between the man and the moment, that 'the creative power has, for its happy exercise, appointed elements, and those elements are not in its own control'. Something much more than the projection of the self was needed.

In view of the importance of this notion of Matthew Arnold's, and its educational implications, it would be well to examine it a little more closely. Arnold was aware that, in a sense, the only sort of environment which could be vital in his own day was what might be termed a substitute environment. Genuine creative literary genius, he thought, lay 'in the faculty of being happily inspired by a certain intellectual and spiritual atmosphere, by a certain order of ideas, when it finds itself in them. . . . But it must have the atmosphere, it must find itself amidst the order of ideas, in order to work freely.' And as Arnold was only too well aware, 'these it is not so easy to command'. Certainly, they were not commanded in mid-Victorian England. Hence the importance of books and reading. Arnold was quite clear that sustained reading was only a substitute, that what was really required was a society 'permeated by fresh thought, intelligent and alive . . . all the books and reading in the world are only valuable as they are helps to this'. But, and at the present day, when there is little likelihood of a national resurgence of vitality of the sort Arnold desired, this seems a point worth insisting on, 'books and reading may enable a man to construct a kind of semblance of it in his own mind, a world of knowledge and intelligence in which he may live and work'.

Hence the need for the exercise of the critical intelligence, to help in the creation of a 'quickening and sustaining atmosphere'. Hence, too, the necessity of a centre of enlightened opinion, that would help to sustain this atmosphere, and to correct the 'provinciality' that marred so many of the ideas and so much of the expression of English writers:

'The less a literature has felt the influence of a supposed centre of correct information, correct judgment, correct taste, the more we shall find in it this note of provinciality. . . . The note of provinciality from want of a centre of correct taste is still more visible, and it is still more common. For here great—even the greatest—powers of mind most fail a man. Great powers of mind will make him inform himself thoroughly, great powers of mind will make him think profoundly, even with ignorance and platitude all around him; but not even great powers of mind will keep his taste and style perfectly sound and sure, if he is left too much to himself, with no "sovereign organ of opinion" in these matters, near him.'

Now Arnold makes it quite clear that it is not only the comparatively narrow field of literary composition and taste that is impoverished by the absence of some such centre as he recommends. The whole of social life, the whole of living needs to be constantly freshened by a continual influx of new and fresh ideas. For it is important to insist once more that Arnold's conception of culture was ultimately pragmatic (in contrast to Newman's idea of liberal knowledge as knowledge 'independent of sequel', which stands on its own pretensions), even if his pragmatic aim included elements that the pragmatic thinkers proper would hardly have acquiesced in.

He was aware of the necessity of a certain detachment from the social scene. The significance of this, however, must now be made clearer.

'Criticism,' he 'argued, must maintain its independence of the practical spirit and its aims. Even with well-meant efforts of the practical spirit it must express dissatisfaction, if in the sphere of the ideal they seem impoverishing and limiting. It must not hurry on to the goal because of its practical importance. It must be patient and know how to wait; and flexible, and know how to attach itself to things and how to withdraw from them.'

Moreover, he was concerned to stress the notion of culture as an inward condition, a necessary attribute of being: 'culture . . . places human perfection in an *internal* condition, in the growth and predominance of our humanity proper, as distinguished from our animality.'

Yet in spite of this insistence on detachment and inwardness, the man of culture was to be no idler, as we have seen. Arnold's conception of society was a larger one than might be allowed by the practical minds of the age. His view of culture, as Dr. Connell in a recent book[1] rightly points out, was a dynamic one: 'Not a having and a resting, but a growing and a becoming is the character of perfection as culture conceives it.' And so 'perfection, as culture conceives it, is not possible while the individual remains isolated. The individual is required, under pain of being stunted and enfeebled in his own development if he disobeys, to carry others along with him in his march towards perfection, to be continually doing all he can to enlarge and increase the volume of the human stream sweeping thitherward.' And it must not be forgotten that 'men of culture are the true apostles of equality'. The aim was to 'make reason and the will of God *prevail*'. It was to further the accomplishment of this aim that the man of culture was to stand aside from many of the more immediate demands for social activity, *reculer pour mieux sauter*, as it were. Arnold's ideal was analagous to that of the Guru in L. H. Myers's *Pool of Vishnu*: 'Into loneliness the spirit by its nature swings; and as it is only in communion and action that man learns, so it is only in loneliness that he discovers what he has learnt. Nevertheless, from his solitude—yes, and from communion—man must always return.' It is perhaps a fault in Arnold, about which more will have to be said later,

[1] W. F. Connell: *The Educational Thought and Influence of Matthew Arnold.*

that he understressed the necessity of learning from communion and action. But it is important that he realized that those who can best serve the world are those who are capable of abstracting themselves from immediate experience, in order to gain a vantage point from which a problem could be seen in a wider context. It was, perhaps, part of the price to pay for the steadiness of view, the check against rash and ill-regulated action that there was sometimes a danger lest remoteness might lead to a certain misconstruing.

It is this capacity for detachment, for seeing that culture was not a matter of selfish ease, but was directly related to the *quality* of living at any one time, for realizing that problems of quality were not irrelevant in a society that was concerned more and more to stress action for action's sake, that marks out Arnold's significant contribution to the problem of education. And lest it should seem that such matters are remote from the everyday concerns of educationalists, a comparison of Arnold's position with that of John Dewey will perhaps bring out the significance of Arnold's view for us to-day. There is indeed a certain relevance in the comparison, for Dewey represents an aspect of that Americanization which, as we have seen, Arnold so feared and condemned.

The two are not divided by any fundamental divergence of aim; for both regard social action, variously conceived, as the ultimate purpose of education. What divides them lies in Arnold's appreciation of the extent to which 'becoming' (social action) is enriched by the nature of 'being' (the richness of the individual's understanding). And something of the measure of the difference between the two can be seen in the difference of stress that they place on the value of the inner life.

We have already noted the emphasis Arnold placed on 'being'; only by a personal enrichment could the individual in turn enrich the society of his time, by enabling him to turn on to it a stream of new and fresh ideas. But such an enrichment implied a temporary withdrawal, a detachment. It is obvious that Dewey is much more nearly involved in the immediacies of the social process than is Arnold:

'The idea of perfecting an "inner" personality is a sure sign of social divisions. What is called inner is simply that which does not connect with others—which is not capable of free and full communication. What is termed spiritual culture has usually been futile, with something rotten about it, just because it has been conceived as a thing which a man might have internally— and therefore exclusively. What one is as a person is what one is as associated with others, in a free give and take of intercourse.'[1]

The important sentence is the last one. To Dewey, the valid personality is one which involves a constant surrender of 'being' to 'becoming', of 'inner' personality to social process; for he will allow the individual no valid state of being other than that acquired in the social intercourse of 'free and full communication'. Dewey's notions are based on his assumption that democracy, conceived as a 'mode of associated living, of conjoint communicated experience', is the only possible form of government. To this all his ideas on education and social living are geared. The necessity of doing away with all aspects of external authority causes him to define the aims of education as falling within the scope of the educative process instead of being externally conceived: 'in our search for aims in education we are not concerned . . . with finding an end outside of the educative process to which education is subordinate. Our whole conception forbids'; and there is the more general statement already quoted in the first chapter, that 'education . . . is a process of living and not a preparation for future living'. Dewey's use of language is frequently deplorably loose; nevertheless it seems clear from these statements that 'being' has surrendered to 'becoming' and that 'process' (Dewey often uses the terms 'change', 'growth' as well) is all important. This he makes explicit when he states: 'Since education is not a means to living but is identical with the operation of living a life which is fruitful and inherently significant, the only ultimate value that can be set up is just the process of living itself.'

Now such ideas make it difficult to make relevant distinctions

[1] John Dewey: *Democracy and Education.*

94

of value. Dewey is aware that not any and every manifestation of energy is of equal value; but it is difficult to see on what grounds he distinguishes between one activity and another. His standard seems to involve what he calls the 'intrinsic continuity' of the activity, as opposed to a 'mere serial aggregate of acts, first doing one thing and then another'. By 'intrinsic continuity' of an activity he seems to imply purposive activity aiming at a preconceived end, an end preconceived, that is to say, by the person entering into the activity: 'The aim as a foreseen end gives direction to the activity; it is not an idle view of a mere spectator, but influences the steps taken to reach the end.' He expressly cuts out externally imposed ends: 'To talk about an educational aim when approximately each act of a pupil is dictated by the teacher, when the only order in the sequence of his acts is that which comes from the assignment of lessons and the giving of directions by another, is to talk nonsense.' Thus the conceiving of ends is restricted to the capacity of the individual to see possibilities at any one moment; and thus the individual's opportunities for mental growth, for 'being', are seriously curtailed. The antithesis between 'preparation for living' and 'process of living', of course, is a false one.[1] For education as a preparation for living involves a living through such a preparation. There is an ambiguity in the significance of the word 'living'. What Dewey means by 'living' in the phrase 'process of living' is much the same as what Arnold means when he speaks of 'swimming with the stream'; the idea of 'preparation' implies that standing aside from the immediate demands of social action that Arnold's notion of 'detachment' and 'disinterestedness' recommends. The difference is one of degree, not of kind, but it involves a difference of qualitative response to the social situation. Arnold realized that fullness of being led to enrichment of becoming; paradoxically, Dewey who is so concerned with 'process' and 'growth', by his repudiation of 'inner' cultivation, reaps a thinner harvest.

It is for reasons of this sort that Arnold is so important as a corrective. For Arnold realized the distinction which we have

[1] Cf. Chapter One, pp. 20–22.

forgotten, the distinction between mechanical and 'vital' knowledge. He saw quite clearly that certain types of activity, certain social aims were not sufficiently important to be conceived of as ends, but were to be regarded as only means to further, more important ends:

'Faith in machinery is . . . our besetting danger; often in machinery most absurdly disproportioned to the end which this machinery, if it is to do any good at all, is to serve; but always in machinery, as if it had a value in and for itself. What is freedom but machinery? what is population but machinery? what is coal but machinery? what are railroads but machinery? what is wealth but machinery? what are, even, religious organizations but machinery? Now almost every voice in England is accustomed to speak of these things as if they were precious ends in themselves, and therefore had some of the characters of perfection indisputably joined to them.'

In his reports on the curricula of the elementary schools with which, of course, Arnold was in almost daily contact for thirty-five years, he makes the same essential distinctions. It informs the whole spirit with which he approached his work, for he conceived that the 'true aim of schools and instruction is to develop the powers of our mind and give us access to vital knowledge'. Some subjects did this; they were what he calls 'formative', and on the necessity of 'formative' instruction he insists time and time again. In his earliest report he was struck, in examining the pupil teachers, 'with the utter disproportion between the great amount of positive information and the low degree of mental culture which they display'. He made these criticisms because he saw that the bulk of the instruction afforded the pupil teachers had 'nothing of that formative character which in education is demanded. As regards sewing, calculating, writing, spelling, this is evident. They are necessary, they have utility, but they are not formative.' And again: 'The great fault of the instruction in our elementary schools is, that it at most gives to a child the mechanical possession of the instruments of knowledge, but does nothing to *form* him, to put him in the way of making the best possible use of them.' Moreover, he saw that this forming power must adapt itself to the child: 'his age, capacity and school time, must in the end govern our proceedings. Undoubtedly there is a danger at present of his being over-urged and over-worked, of his being taught too many things, and not the best things for him.' He objected to the revised code because it made the job of teaching a mechanical exercise, the aim being not to educate the child but to pass a specific test; in addition it involved a change in the function of the inspector. The real purpose of the inspector's visit, as Arnold saw, was 'to test and quicken the intellectual life of the school'; the new test threw upon the inspector such 'a mass of minute detail' that he no longer had the 'needful freshness and spirit (to conduct the old inspection needed a good deal of spirit)' to perform what Arnold properly regarded as the more vital function.

Thus Arnold displays constantly the capacity of a cultivated mind to make valid distinctions between types of activity, to distinguish between those which serve as means and those which involve vital ends.

'But governing the teacher's whole design of instruction . . . should be the aim of calling forth, by some means or other, in every pupil a sense of pleasurable activity and creation; he should resist being made a mere ladder with "information".'

The phrases 'pleasurable activity', 'creation' have a curiously modern ring; related to Arnold's advocacy of the teaching of English and such formative subjects, they have a validity they often do not possess in the hands of modern educationalists.

'People talk contemptuously of "learning lines by heart" but if a child is brought, as he easily can be brought, to *throw himself into* a piece of poetry, an exercise of creative activity has been set up in him quite different from the effort of learning a list of words to spell, or a list of flesh-making and heat-giving foods, or a list of capes and bays, or a list of reigns and battles . . .'

If it would perhaps be wise to lay less emphasis on actual learning by heart than Arnold advocates, it must be remembered that Arnold stressed the importance of full comprehension of what was being learnt, and the need to consider the standard of what was so chosen. For 'good poetry is formative. . . . But of course the good of poetry is not really got unless the sense of the words is known'. What matters, however, is that Arnold realized that genuine creativity was an attribute of the child *in relation to a particular mental atmosphere*, not a purely personal attribute of the child; so that children nowadays are encouraged to be 'creative' in a vacuum, as it were, without the mental stimulus that only subject matter of value and the direct intervention of the teacher can provide. Hence the importance of Arnold's insistence that the teachers should have a high standard of culture:

'It is . . . sufficiently clear, that the teacher to whom you give only a drudge's training, will do only a drudge's work, and will do it in a drudge's spirit: that in order to ensure good instruction even within narrow limits in a school, you must provide it with a master far superior to his scholars.'

At a time when the advocates of a narrow vocational training in the training colleges are becoming increasingly vocal, Arnold's words deserve the widest currency.

For Arnold, it is important to remember, was the heir to a tradition which saw life in terms of conflict rather than of development; it was a tradition that even in Arnold's day was fading fast before the notion of 'progress', but it still had sufficient vitality for Arnold to see the discrepancy between 'natural' man and 'moral' man, a discrepancy which he expressed in the form of the distinction already referred to between the 'ordinary self' and the 'best self'. Behind such notions is a Christian tradition which stretches back to the Middle Ages, a tradition, which, for instance, gave vitality to Macbeth's speech, 'If 'twere done when 'tis done'. Shakespeare, unlike Arnold, lived at a time which retained a vital conception of evil; by Arnold's day, the notion which had reduced evil-doing to the status of social misdemeanour was already prominent. Arnold himself is a portent; for it is perhaps not unjust to say that the conflicts he deals with are those which affect his taste rather than raise the fundamentals of human existence. This at least is the impression one gets if one compares Arnold to his contemporary, Newman; and Newman's picture of the gentleman in the *Idea of a University*, has a certain relevance to Arnold. In one of Arnold's essays the fact that a girl has murdered her baby and is in custody leads Arnold to shrink from the sentimental picture of pathos that his mind paints for him—he seems almost as much affected by the ugliness of her name 'Wragg' as by the eschatological possibilities of the situation; at least this is what he mentions first. I think Mr. Eliot has something of this sort of thing in mind when he denies to Arnold 'the vision of the horror and the glory'.

Now such considerations do not seem to me entirely irrelevant to an estimate of the importance of Matthew Arnold's views on culture and education. For there is a certain thinness in his experience, a thinness that for instance mars his poetry. Despite the importance of his notion of culture, his conception of culture does not entirely escape a certain restriction of scope. Perhaps it was, as Mr. Eliot has said, that his discipline is 'the discipline of culture, not the discipline of suffering'. Or perhaps his idea of culture, lacking as it is in the notion of suffering, has something too self-consciously self-appraising about it; so that, for instance, what he wanted was only the spread of his own particular type of culture which he seems to have thought capable of indefinite extension ('the men of culture are the true apostles of equality'). Part of Arnold's weakness, too, one suspects, comes from his inability to conceive any authority which transcended the State. The State was to be made up of 'our best selves'; and 'our best self' was 'not manifold and vulgar and unstable, contentious, or ever-varying, but one, and whole and secure, and peaceful'. Now this vision of the best self is not an inspiring one—it is not one that has behind it the 'horror' nor is it much informed by the 'glory'. And to imagine that the action of the State was for some reason likely to prove the action of our best selves was a fallacy that one would hardly have thought modern experience necessary to demonstrate. In any case, one would have thought that 'total perfection'—the aim of Arnold's culture—needs to be informed by a 'self', a spirit more vital and comprehensive than 'noble', 'secure' and 'peaceful' would suggest; in Arnold's notion of 'harmonious self-development', by which such perfection is attained, there is indeed a subtle egotism at work.

His social experience seems oddly restricted, although his inspectatorial duties must have revealed many aspects of social life to him that would have been hidden from his contemporaries. In speaking of the lower classes he says: 'And so they are thrown back upon themselves, upon their beer, their gin, and their *fun*.' In that deprecatory sentence I think we find the clue to the comparative narrowness of Arnold's outlook. It is symptomatic of a state of society where the distinctions between the classes have reached unhealthy proportions; it is symptomatic of a personal outlook which is cut off from seeing the function—the cultural (in a wider sense of the word) function—of the 'fun' in relation to the lives and satisfactions of the people. Other greater writers have not despised the 'fun' of the people; but Arnold's rejection of it gives us an indication of why he never saw the problems of the elementary school children in relation to their background.

Now it is considerations of this sort that go to explain a certain, difficult to define, but none the less insistent, disappointment that one feels, for instance, with Arnold's school reports. They are full of highly intelligent remarks, as a consideration of some of the quotations given above should indicate; and yet there is something lacking. Why is it that one feels that even in Arnold's emphasis on the formative importance of certain studies there is a suspicion of something mechanical in his application of his own principle? He stresses the importance of the study of English; one agrees. He urges adequate standards; again one concurs. And yet, when one asks what English studies in the elementary schools meant to Arnold, one has a feeling of disappointment:

'The animation of mind, the multiplying of ideas, the promptness to connect, in the thoughts, one thing with another, and to illustrate one thing by another, are what are wanted; just what *letters*, as they are called, are supposed to communicate. . . . The grammar paper is that paper in their examination which most directly deals with letters, properly so called, and which best shows us, therefore, the amount of the candidate's hold upon letters, and the chance of his communicating the power of letters to others.

'The candidate has to paraphrase a passage of English poetry, and no exercise can better show his range of ideas and quickness of apprehension. He has to parse and analyse sentences, and no exercise can better show his clearness of understanding and his power of reasoning. He has to answer a few questions about our own language or literature. Altogether, the paper is one which tests his information, judgement, and tastes more thoroughly than any other of his papers tests them.'

After the felicity of the opening, one has a feeling of being let down in the rest of the passage. When one sees the passage of Campbell that these pupil-teachers of eighteen or nineteen are being asked to paraphrase and notes Arnold's comment: 'to paraphrase a few lines such as those from Campbell is as good a proof of general intelligence as any that could be required or given', one's bewilderment increases; even though a little later Arnold inconsistently admits that Campbell's poem has no real merit, and the passage is too hard for the candidates. Arnold inveighs against learning lists of facts by rote; but he constantly urges the necessity of learning poetry by heart, because such an exercise he regards as formative. He is not sufficiently flexible to see that any conception of what is to be considered as 'formative' needs some tempering, at least in accordance with time and place and situation.

It would not be fair to blame Arnold for not knowing as much about the process of learning as we now know as a result of recent and persistent research. It is merely that one wonders why Arnold did not investigate a little more persistently the end products of the system of education he was paid to inspect. An understanding of the child mind was not, after all, beyond the capacity of the Victorians, as George Eliot made clear in *The Mill on the Floss*. Arnold's criticisms, so far as they go, are nearly always felicitous; but he never seems to have attempted to see the system as a whole, or to have seen its relevance to the state of culture that he so accurately and adequately criticized. Why, for instance, is there nothing in Arnold's criticism as radical as those observations quoted in the first chapter of this book, and made by George Bourne, a man who had no intimate knowledge of the educational system, but who saw the effects of the sort of education that even Arnold tended to be too complacent about. To do Arnold justice, he did protest against the teaching of remote and unrelated facts: 'A child who has never heard of Paris or Edinburgh, will tell you the measurements of England in length and breadth, and square mileages, till his tongue is tired'; and there is more of the same sort of comment. But he never saw the system as a whole, never asked, as Bourne had asked and seen, what were the final results for 'culture'. Even more remarkable, there is so little apparent carry-over between Arnold the inspector and Arnold the social critic. For a person who was as interested as Arnold appeared to be in the state of contemporary culture, it is remarkable that he uses none of the detailed and intimate information about the state of mind of the nation that he could have acquired in his almost daily visits to schools and which might have helped both in diagnosis and in recommendation for cure. The one, of course, must have affected the other; and yet to read his social and critical works, one would never guess that Arnold had been for so long an inspector of schools. One is not surprised to read, in Dr. Connell's book, that Arnold never seems to have read any book of educational philosophy. His reports certainly are informed by the spirit that informs his criticism; but in the last resort one has the feeling that he wasn't deeply interested; and one is not surprised to read accounts of the hastiness and superficiality of his inspections.

Between Bourne and Arnold, the difference lies, perhaps, in the degree of warm human sympathy that the two men possessed. Bourne had not as profound a mind as Arnold; but he was deeply interested in people and in the intimacies of daily life. Because of this, he is able to see the effect, in terms of individual lives, of the school system—how unprepared their schooling has left 'the people' to face the problems of the new economy. He can see that a 'few pieces of poetry' have not had the 'formative' effect that Arnold hoped. Arnold sees the breakdown of culture in general terms rather than through the particularized analysis of the failure of incentives and satisfactions that gives Bourne's analysis in *Change in the Village* its validity. To call people Barbarians, Philistines or Populace is insufficient; what one needs to know is what the change-over from domestic to factory economy has meant to the intimate lives of the people, what, in fact, lies *behind* the current emphasis on 'machinery' in Arnold's metaphorical use of the term. Arnold had unique opportunities; one feels disappointed that he did not use them better. His appreciation of intimate effects need in no way have diminished his clear-sighted realization of the need for standards.

It is considerations of this sort that give a certain point to the criticisms of Arnold that Henry Sidgwick, one of the most acute of Victorian minds, printed in *Macmillan's Magazine*, in 1867. He charges Arnold with indefiniteness and vagueness; and he points out the inadequacy of Arnold's treatment of religion:

'Culture diffuses "sweetness and light"; I do not undervalue these blessings; but religion gives fire and strength, and the world wants fire and strength even more than sweetness and light.'

Immediately to the point, he has this to say about Arnold's criticism of action:

'All this criticism of action is very valuable; but it is usually given in excess, just because, I think, culture is a little sore in conscience, is uncomfortably eager to excuse its own evident incapacity for action. Culture is always hinting at a convenient season, that rarely seems to arrive. It is always suggesting one decisive blow that is to be gracefully given; but it is so difficult to strike quite harmoniously and without some derangement of attitude. Hence an instinctive, and I think, irrational discouragement of the action on which less cultivated people are meanwhile spending themselves. For what does action, social action really mean? It means losing oneself in a mass of disagreeable, hard, mechanical details, and trying to influence many dull or careless or bigoted people for the sake of ends that were at first of doubtful brilliancy, and are continually being dimmed and dwarfed by the clouds of conflict.'

For all one's admiration of Arnold, one cannot help appreciating some of the justice of this. A closer study of the 'disagreeable, hard, mechanical details' of the life in the schools, a little more appreciation of the fundamental significance of what was going on, a little more willingness to throw himself into the task of making deep and valid and yet particularized educational judgements, a little more of that enthusiasm which, as Sidgwick points out, religion had and which Arnold's culture deprecated, a profounder sympathy and insight that would have correlated Arnold H.M.I. and Arnold, Prophet of Culture, so that there would have been an even more vital cross-fertilization than there actually was, might have given body and substance to culture and sweetness and light to mechanical details. Arnold might have become the greatest educational reformer this country has known; he had after all an official position. Instead, the reform of education has got into the wrong hands; the influence of comparatively superficial thinkers like Dewey has been too pervasive and thus the revolution in English education that has taken place in the last twenty-five years has lacked that qualitative guidance that only a man like Arnold could have given it.

For education, the immediate work of the classroom, demands an attention to 'disagreeable, hard, mechanical details'; but such details need to be tempered by an imagination that can see them in a context. In education, there is necessary a constant interplay between the here and now (the homework to be set, the exercise to be marked, the lesson to be given) and the fullest possible appreciation of ultimate principles and purposes; so that detail shall have its place within the purpose, and the purpose crystallize itself in terms of relevant detail. At the moment we suffer from a too restricted aim. The discovery by the schools of social purpose could have been invigorating and stimulating; certainly it involved an attempt to meet the situation that George Bourne described. But 'social purpose' is a highly ambiguous phrase and society a highly ambiguous concept. What is needed at the moment is a realization of the importance of qualitative considerations, that 'teaching them to live' (to adapt the title of a recent book) is not sufficient if the spirit that informs the living is a cheap and superficial one. That is why Arnold, despite his weaknesses, is timely and salutary, more timely and salutary perhaps than even when he was alive. For what he was deficient in has more than been made good; and what he has to give was never more needed.

There is, however, a contemporary of Arnold who accepted a standard beyond the purely humanistic, and whose work is informed by a deep respect of the individual and the highest regard for the objective value of human and divine learning. In the work of John Henry Newman human culture finds its place in a hierarchical conception which gives coherence and order to all aspects of knowledge. In terms of particularized literary judgements, he is not Arnold's equal. But he is the prime apologist for his and our own age of the essential 'authority' of learning and culture as a step towards the attainment of the highest of all truths, involving a free though paradoxically necessary assent on the part of the individual. Something of what Arnold lacks, then, will be found in Newman.

CHAPTER FIVE

NEWMAN AND THE POSSIBILITY
OF 'ORDER'

'We are always faced both with the question "what must be destroyed?" and with the question "what must be preserved?" and neither Liberalism nor Conservatism, which are not philosophies and may be merely habits, is enough to guide us.'

—T. S. ELIOT

[I]

' "I have never known a Cambridge man", as a reverent disciple of the prophet lately said to me, "who could appreciate Newman." ' The person addressed was Leslie Stephen; and Stephen goes on to observe that 'We held that our common sense enabled us to appreciate (Newman) only too thoroughly by the dry light of reason and to resist the illusions of romantic sentiment'. It is not perhaps remarkable that Stephen, who found John Stuart Mill 'possessed (of) the merits which we most admired—good, downright, hard logic with a minimum of sentimentalism', should be out of sympathy with the Oxford Movement. 'The embodiment of pure passionless reason', as Stephen calls Mill, does not, admittedly, harmonize well with the follower of St. Ambrose who cried 'Non in dialectia complacuit Deo salvum facere populum suum'. Henry Sidgwick, writing a number of years later, bears out the traditional Cambridge approach to Newman adumbrated by the 'reverent disciple' above when in a letter he said:

'The Cardinal interests me—always has interested me—as a man and a writer rather than a reasoner. I delight in the perfect fit of this thought to its expression, and the rare unforced *individuality* of both; but as a *reasoner* I have never been disposed to take him seriously . . . regarding him as a man whose conclusions have always been influenced primarily by his emotions, and only secondarily by the workings of his subtle and ingenious intellect.'

Yet not all Oxford men were sympathetic to Newman. Mark Pattison, blaming an 'inner force of an inherited pietism of an evangelical type', had been drawn into Tractarianism, which he later accused of having 'desolated Oxford life, and (having) suspended, for an indefinite period, all science, humane letters, and the first strivings of intellectual freedom which had moved in the bosom of Oriel'. The process of his rehabilitation he regarded as a triumph of his 'reason' over the obscurantism of the Movement.

To-day, when one looks back upon the controversies that shook England in the midst of the last century, one feels a little surprised that the man who found the *raison d'être* of the University in the training of human intellect, who protested so vehemently against religion as sentiment rather than knowledge, who complained so strongly that 'In the present day mistiness is the mother of wisdom', should be accused with such persistence of irrationalism and obscurantism. Admittedly he made it plain that he 'had a great dislike of paper logic'; but that did not mean that he was an irrationalist. It merely meant that his conception of what constituted thinking differed from the prevailing rationalist view. It started from different premises; it involved different, and, it could be urged, deeper aspects of the personality. Newman's dislike of paper logic was based on a profounder psychological understanding of the processes by which opinions are come by than his opponents gave him credit for. There was behind his 'grammar of assent' an experience of an intense nature that affected his attitude to the logic of the utilitarians for the rest of his life—his conversion. His understanding of the mental processes which led him to the Catholic position helps us to define the nature of his intellectualism; and in considering his educational thought, an understanding of what he regarded as the function of the intellect is vital.

Following the disclaimer about paper logic just quoted, Newman continues, in the *Apologia*:

'For myself, it was not logic that carried me on; as well might one say that the quicksilver in the barometer changes the weather. It is the concrete being that reasons; pass a number of years, and I find my mind in a new place; how? the whole man moves; paper logic is but the record of it. All the logic in the world would not have made me move faster towards Rome than I did. . . .'

This makes it clear that Newman's exercise of the intellect avoided that element of abstractness which was an unavoidable concomitant of the nineteenth-century rationalist position; the difference is analogous to that pointed out by Mill as existing between the assumptions of Coleridge and Bentham:

'the one demanding the extinction of the institutions and creeds which had hitherto existed; the other that they be made a reality; the one pressing the new doctrines to their utmost consequences; the other reasserting the best meaning & purposes of the old. The first type attained its greatest height in Bentham; the last in Coleridge.'

Coleridge's instinct, as Mill points out, is to ask of received opinion 'What is the meaning of it?' Bentham's propensity was to ask 'Is it true?' One stands inside the experience and seeks to understand and correlate, the other to abstract himself and analyse in accordance with a particularly restricted conception of what counts as evidence.[1] The distinction is one that Mr.

---

[1] John Stuart Mill in his essay on *Bentham*, analyses the narrowness of Bentham's mind that made his philosophical outlook so restricted: 'Bentham's contempt, then, of all other schools of thinkers; his determination to create a philosophy wholly out of the materials furnished by his own mind and by minds like his own; was his first disqualification as a philosopher. His second, was the incompleteness of his own mind as a representative of universal human nature. In many of the most natural and strongest feelings of human nature he had no sympathy; from many of its graver experiences he was

John E. Smith made in the *Cambridge Journal* between the reason that looks for 'unity with the known which characterized the Platonic theory of knowledge' and that reason which seeks 'control over the known leading ultimately to that mastery over nature and history which has been the pride (if not yet the fall) of modern man', and which might be termed Baconian. St. Thomas made a similar distinction when he spoke of the difference between *intellectus* and *ratiocinatio*, and called reason 'the imperfection of the intelligence'. We have seen such imperfection in the work of Professor Mannheim.

Newman's *Grammar of Assent* constitutes an extended commentary on the Coleridgean standpoint; and it takes its validity from the central experience of the conversion, as that conversion is described in the *Apologia*, and quoted above. Newman's conception of what constitutes 'proof' or, to use his own word 'certitude', differs from that of the rationalist because Newman is willing to bring into play aspects of the mind that the rationalists leave out. Newman was not like his Catholic contemporary, Cardinal Cullen;[1] he was willing to accept the truths of science and to encourage scientific research as a means of arriving at conclusions within a particular field of the true. But he realized that it was *un*reasonable to assume 'that all reality (is) confined within the field of sensory experience . . . and that there is no reality that cannot be thus apprehended, or at least deduced by reasoning based on sensory experience'. He saw that scientific rationalism was wrong to require only certain types of proof and accept those as conclusive; because such types of proof involved particular abstractions from the totality of experience, and these had no grounds to be considered of

altogether cut off; and the faculty by which one mind understands a mind different from itself, and throws itself into the feelings of that other mind, was denied him by his deficiency of Imagination.' (*Mill on Bentham and Coleridge*, ed. F. R. Leavis.) Though Stephen finds in Mill the embodiment of 'pure passionless reason', Mill was great enough to see the restrictions under which Bentham's logic inevitably works.

[1] Cullen was the archbishop who invited Newman to Dublin to found a Catholic University in opposition to the Queen's Colleges. He was, however, a man of highly conservative temperament, against intellectualism and any compromise with science.

greater importance than proofs drawn from other manifestations of human experience just as imperative.

Thus Newman takes Locke to task because Locke 'consults
his own ideal of how the mind ought to act, instead of interro-
gating human nature as an existing thing, as it is found in the
world'. Locke is blamed for not going 'by the testimony of
psychological facts'; he proposes an abstract doctrine which
breaks down in face of the 'logic of facts' when he states that
'the strength of assent given to each proposition varies with the
strength of the inference on which the assent follows'. A considerable portion of the *Grammar of Assent* is taken up with
repudiating this notion on psychological grounds that make
logical inference only one of the possible means to assent. For
Locke fails to recognize that it is the 'concrete being that reasons
. . . the whole man moves'. The logician abstracts:

'To him dog or horse is not a thing which he sees, but a mere
name suggesting ideas; and by dog or horse universal he means,
not the aggregate of all individual dogs or horses brought together, but a common aspect, meagre but precise, of all existing or
possible dogs or horses . . . (the logician's) business is not to ascer-
tain facts in the concrete, but to find and dress up middle terms.'

Thus it becomes plain that 'formal logical sequence is not in
fact the method by which we are enabled to become certain of
what is concrete'. The real method is through 'the cumulation
of probabilities . . . probabilities too fine to avail separately,
too subtle and circuitous to be convertible into syllogisms, too
numerous and various for such conversion, even were they convertible'. Indeed, language is an inadequate instrument to
convey the totality of experience.

Thus Newman's position constitutes a protest of the individual
mind in concrete relationship to experience against the abstracted analysis of the Benthamites. 'A proof . . . has always in
it, more or less, an element of the personal.' Thinking to him
was an act of the total personality, in which the intellect played
an important part, but which needed to take in evidence derived
from aspects of the mind outside the purely intellectual. To

speak of degrees of assent in the way in which Locke does is to confuse 'the position of the mind relative to the adoption of a given conclusion and the perception of the relation of that conclusion to a premiss'. Thus Newman *involves* the individual in a conclusion in a manner different from that of the scientific rationalist. To come to a conclusion, for Newman, is necessarily a prelude to action, in the way implied by his own conversion. His method, too, involves a fuller appreciation of the assumptions of thought; in Logic, 'its chain of conclusions hangs loose at both ends; both the point from which the proof should start, and the points at which it should arrive, are beyond its reach; it comes short both of first principles and of concrete issues.'

At the same time it is important to realize that Newman does not despise the use of logic *in its place*. This is made clear in the distinction he makes between a 'real' and a 'notional' assent. A 'real assent' is one made by a shift of the total personality in the manner described in the conversion; 'notional assents' are largely based on intellectual abstractions, grasped by an aspect of the mind only. 'Real assents' usually affect conduct; 'notional assents' usually do not. Yet 'notional assents' have their part to play. The mind makes a 'real assent' to the truths of religion; but it needs the mainstay of a 'notional assent' to the truths of theology to maintain the firmness of assent:

'Theology may stand as a substantive science, though it be without the life of religion; but religion cannot maintain its ground at all without theology.'

In other words, the imagination which accepts the truths of religion needs the intellect as its stay and support; religion as sentiment alone earned Newman's particular condemnation. His teaching, it can be said, sometimes betrays a lack of absolute clarity, so that the boundaries between 'real' and 'notional' assents cannot always be marked out with certainty. But the general drift of his argument is unmistakable.

Again, logic provides a necessary public mode of intercourse between mind and mind. 'It is the great principle of order in our thinking.'

Thus his position seems to me profoundly more subtle than theirs who dealt in 'pure passionless reason'; he manages to combine passion and reason in a unity that enables him to seek for fact and knowledge in realms the utilitarians never dreamt of. Logic he will accept within the limitations which his understanding of the insufficiencies of logic make clear to him. If his exposition lacks the absolute clarity of the logician it is because he is attempting a more fundamental task. He cannot be dismissed in the way in which Henry Sidgwick dismissed him precisely because his reasoning is not something apart from his 'individuality', as Sidgwick makes it appear; his reasoning, that is to say, is not something abstracted from him, but something at once subjective and objective. As Mill said: 'Nobody's synthesis can be more complete than his analysis. If in his survey of human nature and life he has left any element out, then, wheresoever that element exerts any influence, his conclusions will fail, more or less, in their applications.' It is because Newman's survey of human nature was more complete than that of so many of his contemporary naturalists, that the constructions of his thought take into account a wider view of human endeavour. It is because his knowledge of the 'subject' personality, and of aspects of individuality that his opponents tended to neglect, is so rich that his comprehension of 'objects' is much wider than that of his contemporaries; so that he can at once approve of science (seeing, however, the limitations within which the scientist must necessarily work), and at the same time assert the claim of theology to be knowledge. Newman's conception of knowledge, as we shall see, must be thought of in terms of a harmonious assimilation of conflicting claims based on a comprehension of the *inherent nature* of the opposing elements. As A. N. Whitehead has said, quoting the motto *Non in Dialectia* (which incidentally appears on the title page of the *Grammar of Assent*): 'This saying, quoted by Cardinal Newman, should be the motto of every metaphysician. He is seeking, amid the dim recesses of his ape-like consciousness and beyond the reach of dictionary language, for the premises implicit in all reasoning.'

Newman's search, then, starting from an unusually complex

appreciation—unusually complex, that is to say, for the nine-teenth century—of the bases of understanding, enabled him to conceive the various fields of knowledge in terms of their ends, and the coalitions and distinctions which marked the disparity in unity, and the unity underlying separateness which charac-terizes the mental constructions of man, in a way unusual since the Middle Ages. The comparative poverty in experience of Liberal England in the nineteenth century—the sort of poverty that Arnold at once complains and remains a portent of—might be said to arise, at least in part, from the poverty inherent in the accepted convention of proof, of the true. For what is not accepted as 'true', what becomes in Newman's own words, a matter of 'sentiment' or 'mistiness', loses its inherent seriousness, no longer provides an element of tension within the mind and atrophies in the way in which the emotions of Mill and Darwin atrophied. Hence it is that Newman, by accepting dogmas which to so many proclaimed the death of the mind, gained a release rather than a desiccation, a fullness rather than an atten-uation. The discipline he accepted was a discipline that trans-cended the humanistic. The immensity of the tradition within which he placed himself provided him with a perspective, en-abled him to make distinctions and clarifications which were out of the range of his contemporaries. His concept of truth, instead of being narrowed, became immensely wider because, as we have seen, more aspects of the personality were involved in the search for it. By no means all Catholics achieved his largeness; the acceptance of dogma does not necessarily entail such an extension. But an age which, like our own, accepts such limited criteria of the true and the useful and insists on confining its activities within the boundaries suggested by such criteria has no call to criticize the acceptance of notions which seem to it so fantastically irrelevant and yet which within their framework permitted the mind of a Newman to work.

It is interesting to consider, at a time when the word 'dog-matic' is regarded as such a term of abuse, that Newman's dog-matism springs from a profounder humility than the scepticism of the rationalists who attacked him. To the Baconian conception of knowledge as power he contrasts knowledge as acceptance; to Locke's ideal of how the mind ought to act he opposes the acceptance of how it does act. To the sciences which seek to extend their empire in fields beyond their capacity to rule he opposes the conception of the end inherent in the undertaking;[1] above all, to the depredations of the 'subject' he contests the life inherent in the 'object'.[2] Truth, it must be remembered, to Newman was something objective, that could be known. To the general proposition that 'we have no right in philosophy to make any assumption whatever, and that we ought to begin with a universal doubt', he counters by saying that such a position in itself involves assumptions and that 'doubt itself is a positive state'.

'I would rather have to maintain that we ought to begin with believing everything that is offered to our acceptance, than that it is our duty to doubt of everything. The former, indeed, seems to be the true way of learning.'

The *Grammar of Assent* is written to urge the possibility of assent and certitude on grounds other than those of scientific 'proof'.

Newman indeed represents an uncommon manifestation, in the modern world, of an integrated and undivided personality. For him personally, the nineteenth century was no 'iron time of doubts, disputes, distractions, fears'; he did not feel its 'sick hurry, its divided aims'. That does not mean to say that he had never known difficulty and conflict; but such difficulties as he

---

[1] Some such reassertion is profoundly necessary in education to-day, where, under the stimulus of that scientific temper of mind that so pervades our society, method has become so much the centre of the picture—to such an extent, in fact, as almost to usurp the end which the method is intended to subserve. Thus, for instance, in schools to-day one finds children spending an immense amount of time on the making of visual and material aids (wall-charts, cardboard models, etc.) to an extent that almost obliterates the purposes which lie behind the practical work.

[2] Matthew Arnold is making a similar point when he states that '. . . for the creation of a master-work of literature two powers must concur, the power of the man and the power of the moment, and the man is not enough without the moment; the creative power has, for its happy exercise, appointed elements, and those elements are not in its own control.'

had had existed within a stable framework of assumptions; fundamentals were not in question. The *Apologia* shows a remarkable instance of a personality that has grown but not split. His end is inherent in his beginning, in his early apprehension of a Sacramental system and of an Object 'received in faith and love, which renders it reasonable to take probability as sufficient for internal conviction'. The logical (in Newman's meaning of the term) fulfilment of this acceptance led to the act of 1845, and the consistency of the position he afterwards maintained.

His apprehension of life in terms of the Object—of something apart from self and other selves—enables Newman to make his most fundamental criticisms of liberal rationalistic scepticism and therefore of the whole *zeitgeist* of the present age and its conception of the range and behaviour of the intellect. He saw in Benthamite scepticism a detachment of mind which failed to commit the whole being and thus lead to an inflation of self. In such an atmosphere 'conscience becomes what is called a moral sense; the command of duty is a sort of taste . . .' Hence the egotism, the self-assertion and self-esteem all too frequently inherent in the humanistic intellectual position, where men accept their own human kind as their standard, where there is

'nothing objective in their religion . . . they do not look out of themselves, because they do not look through and beyond their own minds to their Maker, but are engrossed in notions of what is due to themselves, to their own dignity and their own consistency'.

In such a world 'sin is not an offence against God, but against human nature'; the process by which sin became reduced to the status of social misdemeanour was well under way in Newman's and Arnold's time as we have said; but Newman is one of the few to appreciate the significance of the move. He sums up his appreciation of the dangers of the 'civilized life' when he accuses his contemporaries of shutting themselves up in themselves: 'they are the victims of an intense self-contemplation.'

This concentration on self, then, constitutes for Newman the danger of the uncommitted intellect. It explains his criticism of the 'aggressive, capricious, untrustworthy intellect', for this was the intellect that saw life in terms of the subject and not of its object, that rested on the private judgement of the individual instead of contemplating the external world with due deference to a reality beyond the individual and the purely social. Such a position explains Newman's early conviction that

'it would be a gain to the country were it vastly more superstitious, more bigoted, more gloomy, more fierce in its religion than at present it shows itself to be';

a conviction of fierceness which he later modified but did not retract. The intellect, in fact, essential though its exercise was, must nevertheless observe due order. It could become a mere vehicle for human egotism unless controlled by a regard for its own proper end and objects.

It is, it seems to me, one of the virtues of Newman's position that it enables us to draw boundaries, make distinctions; we can see objects in terms, not of our subjective impressions, but of their ends within a reassertion of a tradition which avoided, as well as might be at that time, that 'dissociation of sensibility' Mr. T. S. Eliot has characterized as occurring at the beginning of the seventeenth century. This insight enabled Newman to tackle the problem of the self in a way which bears comparison with the great European writers like Dostoevsky, Nietzsche and Ibsen; for he is one of the few Englishmen of the nineteenth and twentieth centuries to question the whole basis of contemporary 'civilisation', and raise the deepest problems of the relationship of the individual ego to the external world. Arnold remained a liberal, though 'tempered by renunciation' as we have seen; and his criticisms of contemporary society remain criticisms of manifestations rather than of assumptions. And Mill, despite his appreciation of Coleridge, remained too much within the tradition of the utilitarians to make any fundamental criticisms. Newman's understanding of the complexity of the mind led him to apprehend the necessary balance between self and not-self. His probings into the evils of the self-contemplating ego matches, though on a more abstract plane, the implications of

Ibsen's 'Troll, to thyself be enough', Dostoevsky's 'All things are lawful' and Nietzsche's rejection of the clown Socrates. Newman, of course, made his criticisms from within the dogmatic structure of the Catholic Church. Whereas the European thinkers had to reconstruct the whole basis of the moral world from their own selves and the wreckage of the European tradition, Newman could invoke the reassertion of a specific tradition. The difference between the two outlooks, indeed, explains the comparative neglect of Newman, outside Catholic circles.[1] For the European thinkers tackled the contemporary dilemma with the age's own weapon, the unattached mind. Thus their solutions are less stable but probe more deeply into the human pysche than did Newman. But their constructions are precarious, depending on the integrity of an individual mind unsupported by any external order; the same is true of Lawrence, too, as we shall come to see. Again, Newman hid his enlightenment, paradoxically enough, in a tradition that to the times stood for obscurantism. He owes his true liberality, perhaps, to the fact that he was a convert, that he stood at once inside and outside the tradition, that he had arrived at Catholic conclusions by processes that stood outside the Catholic purview. (And of course he was not always by any means *persona grata* with other members of the Church.) At Oriel in the 'twenties and 'thirties, the Noetics (as the liberal-minded fellows of the college were called) gave Newman a taste, unique in the Oxford of the day, of the liberalism that called all into question: 'There was a wholesome intellectual ferment maintained in the Oriel common-room of those days', reveals Mark Pattison, who proceeded to Oriel as a very raw undergraduate in 1830; and indeed, Pattison almost suggests that the tractarian reaction came as the 'indispensable, reactionary, and complementary phase' to the 'originality', the 'free discussion' of the Noetics. Newman, then, knew Liberalism at first hand. At the same time, as a Catholic, he was sufficiently outside the Catholicism of the Cullens to avoid the narrowness that unintelligent dogmatism could pro-

---

[1] This is perhaps the moment to point out that this appreciation of Newman is written by a non-Catholic.

duce. It was a combination of these facts that led the great opponent of liberalism to become the high advocate of Liberal Knowledge. And to the explanation of this apparent paradox we must now turn.

[II]

The liberalism that Newman fought so hard and that he analysed so mercilessly in an appendix to the later version of the *Apologia* has gained the day. Even within Newman's lifetime,

'the Liberalism which gives a colour to society now, is very different from that character of thought which bore the name thirty or forty years ago. Now it is scarcely a party; it is the educated lay world.'

It has produced the modern democratic community, 'worm-eaten with Liberalism' to employ Mr. Eliot's phrase. With its triumph has been destroyed the type of education for which Newman fought. Knowledge as an end in itself—I will define the significance of this more fully later—has undergone the double challenge I have already defined: that of knowledge for utility or social purpose, and that of knowledge for expression of self. Both, of course, may be said to emanate from the Baconian conception of Knowledge for Power. The increasing pragmatic emphasis in learning can be traced from Bacon through the Utilitarians and Brougham to Dewey and beyond. The implementation of Dewey's assertion that the 'educational process has two sides—one psychological and one sociological' leaves out of serious account that third term which stands between the individual and society; I refer to that organized body of human knowledge and values, independent of the social purposes of the moment, with which Newman was so much concerned; so that he can speak of education as 'a process steadily carried on through years on fixed principles, towards a definite end; as is its termination, so must have been its beginning, and its continuation is according to its course hitherto', where the stress is rightly laid on the internal logic implicit in the structure of any field of study. Again, in laying down the duties of a professor, he speaks of the need for the

'. . . steady pursuit and thorough mastery of the department of science or learning, which he has undertaken. His main office is to expound and illustrate it; to deepen its principles and to enlarge its stores; and to erect what may be called a real objective image of it, such as may have value in itself, as distinct from the accidents of the day.'

Indeed, Newman's concern for the integrity of the professor's particular field of study went almost further than one could wish; at least the prevailing emphasis is very different from what it is to-day:

'He is not bound by duty, though he may be advantageously induced by circumstances, to adapt himself to his particular hearers, and to bring down his teaching to their capacity: on the other hand, they are required to prepare themselves for what may be at first above them, and to raise themselves towards the level of his view and the standard of his intellect.'

Here then, the value of the 'discipline' is not neglected; the student must fit himself to the necessities of an objective reality, a specific field of study having its own laws and making its own demands. To-day, when Dewey writes that

'with the advent of democracy and modern industrial conditions, it is impossible to foretell definitely just what civilization will be twenty years from now. Hence it is impossible to prepare the child for any precise set of conditions',

he is stating a truism that would hold for any type of civilization, however static; but because of the emphasis it receives in his thought, he becomes blind to the contrary terms in the situation which should counter-balance the notion of process and flux. Thus when Dewey proceeds to say that 'To prepare (the child) for the future life means to give him command of himself', he forgets that one can only gain command of oneself in certain terms, that the self is not automatic but needs to be ordered in relation to certain conceptions, values, notions of conduct which transcend the mere process of day to day living. Now the only criterion of such conceptions and values which Dewey has to offer is, as we have seen, just that of society in its state of constant evolution. Hence if one pushes Dewey's ideas to any sort of conclusion education becomes impossible; because as one moment is never the same as the next, the education that would fit a child for one moment must give way to that which would fit him for the next and so on. Hence there is a complete paralysis of effort, and 'being' merges into the constant flux of 'becoming', in the way we have examined in the last chapter.

In so far as it is possible to extract any sharply defined and clear ideas from the turgidity and looseness of Dewey's expressions, they strike me as providing a logical evolution from nineteenth-century liberalism of the sort that Newman attacked. The dissolution of the notion of belief in belief, the acceptance of only limited and restricted notions of proof, a wholesale scepticism about ideas other than those based on sensory appreciation leads to just that destruction of the world of values that Dewey's making the process of living the end of living implies.

Against this scepticism inherent in the liberal position Newman posits the mastery of 'becoming' by 'being'. And that mastery is not the mastery of power over 'becoming' but the mastery of transcendence. Newman is not ignorant, as we have seen, of the need for an essential 'becoming' on the part of the individual. Man is not born good, but in sin; and Newman stresses the force of Christ's remark 'Who hath ears to hear, let him hear'; he regards belief 'as a state of mind' for which 'a special preparation of mind may be necessary'—for belief generates belief. Hence the individual's capacity to reach certitude depends on his prior capacity to appreciate its necessity.[1] This, of course, is quite consistent with the view of Christian responsibility. What has not to be forgotten, however, is that

[1] Thus it is interesting to note that *The Grammar of Assent* was not written to convert, but to provide the converted with arguments with which to confute the rationalistic liberalism of the day.

truth is something objective and can be achieved. And that truth contains a vast complex of elements; the achievement of a life in purely social terms, which is the purpose and aim of Dewey's system, is to Newman merely a by-product, not to be ignored but not to be over-stressed, in the attainment of an end which far transcends the claims of society.[1]

It is significant that Newman should call his great educational work *The Idea of a University*; for such a title implies that the Idea should guide the physical manifestation. He thus considers knowledge in terms of its end, in the Aristotelian manner. For Newman, the function of a university education lies in the training of the intellect:

'This process of training, by which the intellect, instead of being formed or sacrificed to some particular or accidental purpose, some specific trade or profession, or study or science, is disciplined for its own sake, for the perception of its own proper object, and for its own highest culture, is called Liberal Education.'

and again 'Truth of whatever kind is the proper object of the intellect'.

Now it is remarks of this kind that cause raising of eyebrows by modern educationalists. The idea that the intellect or any part of the mind could have an object other than that concerned with the social purposes of the day ('swimming with the stream', to use Arnold's phrase) is one, as we have seen, that would be explicitly denied by many modern thinkers. But once accept Newman's premises, which, as we have seen, are bound up with a particular conception of human nature and which, in the terms within which they are expressed, no rationalist could in

---

[1] Thus, though the final aims of education are based on unchangeable, 'given' truths, Newman regards education as being concerned with 'questions not merely of immutable truth, but of practice and experience'. An interesting account of how Newman showed himself capable of the day to day business of university life and of how he manages to integrate his immediate problems with his fundamental principles can be gleaned from Fergal McGrath's *Newman's University: Idea and Reality*, which appeared after this essay had been written.

any case disprove, the rest follows quite naturally. The force of making the intellect have its own end comes in the denial that it is formed 'to some particular or accidental purpose'; and the idea of 'its own sake' must be read in conjunction with that denial of accidental social purpose. Even if one were to deny the whole set of Newman's assumptions, one could find no other set which would fit the evidences of Newman's understanding of the mind better; and such understanding, in that it springs from the concrete actualities of a particular mind, cannot be brushed aside. The only alternative is a scepticism based on individual denials of experience, one whose results can be seen in the comparative lack of richness in our conception of human personality over the last two hundred years (at least) and which leaves the dilemma of the ego unsolved. Behind Newman's notion lies the residue of mystery—*abeunt omnia in mysterium*; and no better solution to the problem of human ends has been found. Yet in saying this one must not forget that definition of the mystery which is theology and which Newman is concerned to insist on as *knowledge*.

At the same time it must be remembered that Newman did not deny the possible usefulness that would accrue from this training of the intellect; such utility might be incidental but it would be none the less real. To the Cullens of the Catholic world, who were so little concerned about the intellectual capacity of their priests, Newman maintained that he wanted 'the educated layman to be religious and the devout ecclesiastic to be intellectual'. He was quite certain that the Church stood in no danger from the advancement of knowledge:

'. . . if anything seems to be proved by astronomer, or geologist, or chronologist, or antiquarian, or ethnologist, in contradiction to the dogmas of faith, that point will eventually turn out, first, *not* to be proved, or, secondly not *contradictory*, or thirdly, not contradictory to anything *really revealed*, but to something which has been confused with Revelation.'

Hence his desire 'to stand on good terms with all kinds of knowledge'; and hence his contention that, in scientific investigation, 'the investigator should be free, independent, unshackled in his movements; that he should be allowed . . . without impediment, to fix his mind intently, nay exclusively, on his special subject, without the risk of being distracted every other minute in the process and progress of his inquiry, by charges of temerariousness, or by warnings against extravagance or scandal.

Thus, though Newman is concerned to invoke a tradition, it is not in dead or static terms. It is for reasons of this sort that Newman is justified in his appellation 'Liberal Knowledge'. He takes all knowledge as his province, harmonizing the various claims of the sciences and arts in terms of their natures, of the ends they are intended to subserve. Those ends have, as it were, an incidental utility; yet this incidental utility is, in fact, more potentially powerful in the shaping of social action than modern 'education for life' would be. For the pragmatist tackles each problem as it arises; and he conceives it as it arises. He fails to realize that his very capacity to conceive it depends upon the anterior capacity to make the relevant distinctions which will appreciate a problem in its relational significance. A problem is not an abstract entity but an organic configuration with its affiliations to 'before' and 'after'. The capacity of the mind to see the 'problem', then, depends on the subtlety of its appreciation of the full structure of the problem and its relations.

It is for reasons such as these that one finds Newman's ability to conceive the significance of human knowledge in relation to the totality of life so much richer than that of most other nineteenth- and twentieth-century educationalists. A philosophy which accepts the 'process of living' as an end in itself must accept any and every manifestation of living, if it is to be at all consistent. In actual fact, Dewey depends on the anterior acceptance of much of the traditional morality of the times to save him from the moral and social anarchy endemic in his theories; but he shows little awareness of his assumption. Newman, on the other hand, by conceiving ends beyond the mere 'process' of life, can see the necessity of controlling any and every manifestation of vitality in terms of those higher purposes.

Thus, when Newman sees a purpose to knowledge beyond that of mere utility, he serves the purpose of utility better than the utilitarians themselves do. One must admit his claim:

'I say that a cultivated intellect, because it is a good in itself, brings with it a power and a grace to every work and occupation which it undertakes, and enables us to be more useful, and to a greater number.'[1]

Moreover, Newman's appreciation of the ends inherent in any organized science or body of knowledge enables him to make distinctions and discriminations between the capacities of the various subject bodies and their proper relevances in the world of fact and activity. Nothing is more distressing in the modern world than the way in which specialists within one field usurp the functions of specialists in other fields. At a popular level this manifests itself in the way in which popular figures of the day are willing to pronounce on any variety of subjects quite outside their trained capacity to do so. At a profounder stage, it is seen in encroachments of scientists on the province of the philosopher, encroachments of the sort that the late Susan Stebbing drew attention to in her book *Philosophy and the Physicists*, where she commented on the unfortunate pronouncements of Jeans and Eddington in fields in which they were not qualified to give opinions.[2] A most serious usurpation can be seen at the present day in the manner in which political notions have invaded fields in which they are not relevant . . . the world of

---

[1] And this despite those who deprecate the idea of transfer of training. For in assessing such transfer educationalists are mostly concerned with the *mechanics* of learning and not with that 'illumination', to use Newman's word, which can be derived from certain types of knowledge and which can be profitably transferred to light up another field of study.

[2] Cf. too, Mr. Stephen Toulmin's protest in a recent broadcast talk: '. . . when we begin to expect from the scientist a tidy, simple—especially an all-purpose—picture of the world; when we treat his tentative and carefully qualified conclusions as universal certainties; when we inflate some discovery of limited scope into the mainspring of the universe, and try to read in the scientist's palm the solutions of difficult problems in ethics, aesthetics, politics or philosophy; then we are asking of him things he is in no position to give, and turning his theories into myths.'

learning has already been instanced. Newman himself shows how political and scientific notions have reduced God to the role of constitutional monarch; so that religion has become a matter of sentiment, and God 'but a function or correlation or subjective reflection and mental impression of each pheno- menon of the material or moral world, as it flits by us', instead of an Object.

It is because Newman saw that 'coalitions and comprehen- sions for an object have their life in the prosecution of that object and cease to have meaning as soon as that object is comprom- ised or disparaged' that he is able to avoid those improper encroachments which spring ultimately from the arrogant usurpations of the subject. Newman apprehends the uniqueness of human personality as something over against, but given validity by, the living reality of God, the Object, not in the mere existence of man, the subject; and thus Newman's idea of in- tegration, wholeness, to employ words that are so bandied about nowadays, was in terms of an objective reality, not in the mere expansion of a 'subject'.

This naturally affects Newman's conception of the whole circle of human knowledge, which exists as at once an objective challenge and a temptation to man. For knowledge must keep its own bounds, like anything else; and the threat of civilized knowledge lay in the emanation of the secularized humanized gentleman, with the inadequacy of make up that Newman so acutely analyses.[1] Nevertheless, divine knowledge, as Newman realized, 'depended' on human knowledge; just as human knowledge depended for its right ordering on that of the divine. It is one of Newman's most acute appreciations that, 'you will soon break up into fragments the whole circle of secular know- ledge if you begin the mutilation with divine'. Divine knowledge was the keystone to the arch; to it all the others were bound and it kept all the others in their rightful positions. Newman's conception of human knowledge is at once of fruitful interpene- tration and of careful discrimination. He conceives the univer-

[1] 'Liberal Education makes not the Christian, not the Catholic, but the gentleman.'

sity as being concerned with universal knowledge, a meaning of the term which historical investigation has not borne out; but his Idea, of course, is not invalidated because of an historical inaccuracy; his university merely dissociates itself from any particular university and becomes instead an Apology for Universal Knowledge.

This universal knowledge, then, is an objective entity apart from the realizing subject; and Newman's integrations take place in terms of that object. Modern attempts at integration almost always take place in terms of the subject; so that 'total education', Mr. M. L. Jacks exuberantly proclaims, will have as its immediate aims the 'providing the whole child with a wholly satisfying life the whole of its time, at making each school day an intelligible and significant whole, in which all needs, physical, moral, intellectual and spiritual, will be wholly met and integrated'. Perhaps comment could be excused. Wholeness in such terms, of course, is almost meaningless; the problem of evil disappears, and criteria by which the 'wholeness' could be judged are non-existent. The quotation is only interesting as showing the fantastic lengths to which modern subjectivism can go.

Newman realized that all sciences are abstractions, and that all are subject to 'that imperfection, which ever must attend the abstract when it would determine the concrete'. Hence it is necessary to insist that

'all the sciences come to us as one, that they all relate to one and the same subject-matter, that each separately is more or less an abstraction, wholly true as an hypothesis, but not wholly trustworthy in the concrete . . . needing the support and guarantee of its sister sciences, and giving in turn while it takes.'

This arises, of course, from Newman's belief that 'the universe in its length and breadth is so intimately knit together, that we cannot separate off portion from portion, and operation from operation, except by a mental abstraction'.

Thus all sciences at once 'need and subserve each other'. Each science is an abstraction that goes to make up some part of the concrete whole; each science needs the rest to complete the picture of that whole; and finally

'it is not every science which equally, nor any one which fully, enlightens the mind in the knowledge of things as they are, or brings home to it the external object on which it wishes to gaze. Thus they differ in importance'.

The subject, the viewing mind

'advances towards the accurate apprehension of (the objective truth) in proportion to the number of sciences which it has mastered; and which, when certain sciences are away, in such a case has but a defective apprehension, in proportion to the value of the sciences which are thus wanting, and the importance of the field on which they are employed'.

Thus the onus of making the effort to grapple with the external world, which exists as a concrete fact in the totality of sciences, is thrust upon the subject; and thus Newman's education, for all its appreciation of a hierarchy of value, is an education of acceptance and humility. It is an education, not in terms of a subjective 'need', but in terms of an objective necessity. There is, he says

'no true culture without acquirements, and . . . philosophy presupposes knowledge. It requires a great deal of reading or a wide range of information, to warrant us putting forth our opinions on any serious subject'.

Hence it is necessary to accept the findings of those who have gone before with a certain degree of humility; those who rely on their own resources may gain popularity for a time, but their readers 'will find in the long run that (their) doctrines are mere theories . . . that they are chaff instead of bread' and they will be rejected.[1]

[1] That, of course, does not prevent the acceptance of many false prophets —inevitable in a society in which, as Newman said of his own day '. . . authority, prescription, tradition, habit, moral instinct and the divine influences go for nothing, in which patience of thought, and depth and consistency of view, are scorned as subtle and scholastic, in which free discussion and

Hence, too, in Newman's scheme, the acquiring of knowledge requires effort, effort in the acquiring of the 'object':

'We know, not by a direct and simple vision, not at a glance but, as it were, by piecemeal and accumulation, by a mental process, by going round an object, by the comparison, the combination, the mutual correction, the continual adoption of many partial notions, by the joint application and concentration upon it of many faculties and exercises of the mind.'

In contradistinction to the subjectivist modern notions of the 'spontaneous' he stresses the need for training: 'the eye of the mind, of which the object is truth, is the work of discipline and habit.' At the same time, and this must be emphasized, he realizes how vital it is that the mind shall co-operate in the undertaking, so that there shall be a genuine coalescence of subject and object:

'The enlargement consists, not merely in the passive reception into the mind of a number of ideas hitherto unknown to it, but in the mind's energetic and simultaneous action upon and towards and among those new ideas, which are rushing in upon it.'

Information, collections of facts are not education; what is needed is the action of a 'formative power, reducing to order and meaning the matter of our acquirements'. Thus education implied the 'making the objects of our knowledge subjectively our own. . . . There is no enlargement, unless there is a comparison of ideas one with another, as they come before the mind, and a systematizing of them. . . It is not a mere addition to our knowledge which is the illumination.' And he sternly combats the modern error of distracting and enfeebling the mind by an unmeaning profusion of subject-fields for study.

Newman, then, accepts the best feature of modern educational thought by conceiving the mind as an activity and by rejecting

fallible judgment are prized as the birthright of each individual'. One need not be so forthright in disparaging free discussion and yet see the force of Newman's criticism.

the acquisition of facts *as such* as in any way constituting a valid education. But he realizes that the mind can only develop if it works on substance of value outside itself. Thus he avoids that emphasis on the 'inner' which, as we have seen, mars the psychology of Froebel and which so many modern educationalists have adopted. Again his conception of objects transcends the social purposes of the day, and thus places aims of social utility in their right perspective; indeed, as I have shown, he enriches our apprehension of such aims by enabling us to see them in a perspective which transcends their incidence and context.

Thus Newman remains the critic of those who would counter the Gradgrind approach by the doctrines of self-expression or social purpose. He is with them to the extent of condemning the acquisition of unrelated facts; he criticizes nineteenth-century education because 'all things now are to be learned at once, not first one thing and then another, not one well but many badly', and condemns the 'dissipation of mind' that goes with the senseless proliferation of reading matter, as if the population were 'to be passively, almost unconsciously enlightened by the mere multiplication and dissemination of volumes'. But when he condemns the idea that 'learning is to be without exertion, without attention, without toil', he unconsciously hits at a radical defect in the modern movement. For the implementation of his own positive educational standards arose out of the reassertion of the European tradition of learning and the resuscitation of the life inherent in the objective enterprise of learning, as against that collapse of the tradition which is implied, it is necessary to repeat, in the modern finding of objects worthy of pursuit, either within the self or inside the impoverished social processes of the day.[1] Newman's assertion that 'knowledge . . . is the indispens-

---

[1] Thus educationalists, to-day, exalt either self-expression or, more recently, group techniques of learning. The former finds its purpose in the 'needs' of the individual, the latter in the 'needs' of society—'getting on together' and such-like aims. In both cases, the end has tended to become something other than learning itself, despite the fact that to assess the 'needs' of either the individual or society, a great deal of what Newman calls 'philosophy' or 'illumination' is essential; and this 'illumination' can only be acquired through the type of learning Newman is concerned to recommend.

able condition of expansion of mind, and the instrument of attaining it', within the framework of the conceptions of knowledge and expansion of mind we have here examined, never needed more insisting on than it does to-day. For if knowledge has its temptation in that, 'viewed as Knowledge, (it) exerts a subtle influence in throwing us back upon ourselves, and making us our own centre, and our minds the measure of all things', at least an intellectual cultivation, which implies training and law of a kind, is one road by which we can escape the dangers of 'passion and self-will'. In an age which has seen so much of that egocentricity which emanates from making man the measure of all things, the theocentricity of Newman's system, combined with the subtlety of his inner psychological appreciation, deserves more of a hearing than it gets. In the terms in which he expresses it, the tradition he urges is seen still to have the possibilities of life despite what three centuries of 'private judgement' have produced. For Newman replaced the negative scepticism of liberalism by a positive conception of a Liberal Knowledge which, even for the Protestant, is valid because it transcends the possible and actual narrowness of the dogmatic system within which the notion was conceived. If, more than anything else in education to-day, we need the reassertion of a tradition of (objective) value that will transcend the individual and social purposes of man, it is not necessary to have accepted the Catholic dogmatic system before one can see that Newman has pointed a way.

One point remains to add. In view of the strictures passed on Arnold in the last chapter, about his lack of personal concern for, and interest in, the children, it is important to note how much Newman emphasized the need for individual understanding between teacher and pupil. He was a strong supporter of the collegiate system, so that the tutor could exercise a direct influence on the student; and in his paper on *Discipline and Influence*, he makes it clear on which he wishes the emphasis to lie. To a friend who accuses him of making 'more of *persons* than is just, and not laying stress enough upon order, system and rule', he admits that personal influence is not enough for the well-being of the University, though 'it is indeed its essence', and that 'something more is necessary than barely to get on from day to day; for its sure and comfortable existence we must look to law, rule, order.' Yet however important Discipline is, Influence must precede:

'I say then, that the personal influence of the teacher is able in some sort to dispense with an academic system, but that the system cannot in any sort dispense with personal influence. With influence there is life, without it there is none; if influence is deprived of its due position, it will not by those means be got rid of, it will break out irregularly, dangerously. An academic system without the personal influence of teachers upon pupils, is an arctic winter; it will create an ice-bound, petrified, cast-iron University, and nothing else.'

It must be remembered, of course, that this was at a time when university discipline was very oppressive—when going to plays and hunting in pink were forbidden.[1] To-day, when 'Influence', of a sort, is so pervasive, and 'Discipline', of any sort, so weak, it is to be doubted whether Newman would have maintained his relative emphasis between the two. Nevertheless, that he represented a kindly tolerance and understanding of young people not always usual in his day, and that he realized the delicacy of the problem of university discipline is certain:

'It is easy enough to lay down the law and to justify it, to make your rule and keep it; but it is quite a science, I may say, to maintain a persevering, gentle oversight, to use a minute discretion, to adapt your treatment to the particular case, to go just as far as you safely may with each mind, and no further, and to do all this with no selfish ends, with no sacrifice of sincerity and frankness, and with no suspicion of partiality.'[2]

[1] Cf. Fergal McGrath, op. cit., p. 336–8.
[2] *Campaign*, report for year 1854–5. Quoted McGrath, op. cit., p. 340. The whole long extract that Dr. McGrath gives is well worth reading, for it shows how carefully Newman had considered the problem.

This, too, is sufficient to temper any suspicion of rigidity in his dealings, and to show that it is possible to combine certainty of standards and a high sense of intellectual mission with flexibility of personal approach and genuine concern for individuals.

Despite, however, Newman's concern for the individual, which is so marked a feature of his administration, his penetration into the human psyche is obviously not as detailed, nor as profound as that of a more modern writer, D. H. Lawrence. In order, then, to clarify still further the idea of the 'freedom' of the individual, it is necessary to examine Lawrence's position.

CHAPTER SIX

D. H. LAWRENCE AND THE NATURE
OF FREEDOM

*'Life in society is a sort of secondary or regenerate life that has
to struggle with the old Adam; and this old Adam, like all animal
and primitive forces, denies that he is justly subordinated, and
on the contrary feels deeply that his is the brave, the pure, the
free ideal, and that in trampling upon him circumstances and
conventions are smothering a soul: a feeling that here and there
breaks out into mystic and passionate rebellions.'*
—GEORGE SANTAYANA: *Obiter Scripta*

[I]

There are probably at least half a dozen Lawrences;
and certainly two of them are relevant to a consideration of his educational ideas. There is the Lawrence
of untrammelled assertion and isolation. 'You tell me
I am wrong. Who are you, who is anybody to tell me I am
wrong? I am not wrong.' And there is the Lawrence who sought
vital connection and belongingness: 'Thank God I'm not free,
any more than a rooted tree is free.' These two Lawrences, as
we shall see, are merely two sides of a fundamentally coherent
personality—a personality with a true centrality, a deep, *rooted*
individuality. But in his early days, the two aspects seem to
emerge, in his dealings with his classes, as two unrelated moods.
As all the world knows, Lawrence was a trained teacher, and
taught for a couple of years at Davidson Road School, Croydon,
between 1910 and 1912. On the whole he disliked teaching:
'You have no idea what a nightmare it is to me, now I have
escaped', he wrote to A. W. McLeod, a former colleague, after

illness had forced him to leave teaching for ever; though, incidentally, he left with admirable testimonials.[1] He has left us some record of his feelings as a schoolmaster in his poems and letters; and in two of these poems, his delighted sense of relatedness and connection with his class and the contrary feeling of disruption and rejection emerge very clearly. In *The Best of School*, Lawrence speaks of relationship:

> *This morning, sweet it is*
> *To feel the lads' looks light on me . . .*
>
> *Touch after touch I feel on me*
> *As their eyes glance at me for the grain*
> *Of rigour they taste delightedly.*
> *As tendrils reach out yearningly,*
> *Slowly rotate till they touch the tree*
> *That they cleave unto, and up which they climb*
> *Up to their lives—so they to me.*
>
> *I feel them cling and cleave to me*
> *As vines going eagerly up; they twine*
> *My life with other leaves, my time*
> *Is hidden in theirs, their thrills are mine.*

It is interesting to note Lawrence's use of the tree image—it is one he returned to frequently. Just as significant, perhaps, is the relationship he defines between himself and the boys—a suspicion of the clinging, mutual parasitism ('their thrills are mine') that he was later to repudiate so vehemently. But a little later, when he had reached the *Last Lesson of the Afternoon*, there is a significant difference of tone: 'When will the bell ring, and end this weariness.' The young tendrils have become a 'pack of unruly hounds'.

> *What does it matter to me, if they can write*
> *A description of a dog, or if they can't?*
> *What is the point? To us both, it is all my aunt!*
> *And yet I'm supposed to care, with all my might.*

[1] Cf. *Early Life of D. H. Lawrence*, by Ada Lawrence and Stuart Gelder.

> *I do not, and will not; they won't and they don't;*
>   *and that's all!*
> *I shall keep my strength for myself; they can keep*
>   *theirs as well.*
> *Why should we beat our heads against the wall*
> *Of each other? I shall sit and wait for the bell.*

Both reactions are typical of Lawrence; both, in fact, are reactions, responses out of his vital self; both, in their as yet immature way, bear witness to that power which, as Dr. Leavis points out, Lawrence shared with Blake; he had 'the same gift of knowing what he was interested in, the same power of distinguishing his own feelings and emotions from conventional sentiment, the same "terrifying honesty" '.[1] In his acceptances and in his rejections, Lawrence starts with himself and his *deep* personal life; what evolves, about education or anything else, emerges from his own deepest naked and unashamed feelings; and it is because he has a genius for insight, possessed by very few people and because he has the great artist's gift of projecting and making 'impersonal' that insight—in the novels—that he attains the profoundest understanding of the modern dilemma —an understanding, however, which is not content to rest in negatives—of practically any writer of our day. In an age given over to the abstract and the generality, Lawrence has that marvellous gift of concreteness and immediacy which gives his criticism of the system—the 'certain moral scheme'[2] of Dostoevsky and Tolstoi, for instance—its validity. He has the rich closeness to experience of the *gamin*. In his *Fantasia*, for instance, he catches the immediate tones of the sickly loving mother with unerring accuracy: 'You see, dear, one day you'll love a man as I love Daddy, more than anything else in the *whole* world,' etc. (He was, of course, a wonderful mimic.) Many of his essays have the rich exuberance, drama and *humour*, the living speech be-

[1] It will be obvious in the ensuing that I owe a great deal to Dr. F. R. Leavis's profound studies of Lawrence—first in *For Continuity*, from which the above quotation is taken, and then, more recently, in *Scrutiny*. Perhaps this acknowledgement will suffice.

[2] D. H. Lawrence: *Letters*.

hind them, that sometimes reminds one of Shakespeare's great irreverent fools—though to say that is to suggest that Lawrence's wonderful clarity of vision is, like that of Lear's Fool, only negative; whereas his criticism, it is necessary to insist, is counterbalanced by a triumphant positive assertion. The quickness of his imagery, however, can be low-life Shakespearian: 'This bit, I admit, is bordering on mysticism. I'm sorry, because I don't like mysticism. It has no trousers and no trousers' seat: *n'a pas de quoi.*'

Now it is this concreteness that makes his thinking on educational matters so vital. There is, behind his writings on educacation, as we shall see, a great deal of memory and bitter experience; and in that sense, as often in Lawrence (and haven't the biographers seized their opportunity!) his 'thinking' is deeply personal. But, because of his deep honesty and his individual integrity, because what he stood for as a person and what he saw has in it the stuff of health, honesty and vitality, he not only helps to clear away a great deal of the dead wood which hinders the growth of the sort of personality he looked for and that our civilization so cruelly hinders, but also suggests a positive 'freedom' that commands our assent in its complex emergence from the psychic depths of his understanding.

Lawrence's specifically educational ideas, as may perhaps be guessed from the foregoing, need to be considered in the context of his general criticism of our modern life. Education to Lawrence was not a matter of fiddling with curricula—he repudiated 'smatterings'—or a hankering after 'methods' that only serves to hide a basic uncertainty; it necessitated a fundamental reorientation of the total human personality. In *St. Mawr* we read:

'And every civilization, when it loses its inward vision and its cleaner energy, falls into a new sort of sordidness, more vast and more stupendous than the old savage sort. An Augean stables of metallic filth.

'And all the time, man has to arouse himself afresh, to cleanse the new accumulations of refuse. To win from the crude wild nature the victory and the power to make a new start, and to cleanse behind him the century-deep deposits of layer upon layer of refuse: even of tin cans.'

(How the vital detail about tin cans conjures up Dickens; but Lawrence has the vitality of a Dickens from the *inside*.[1]) The 'layers upon layers of refuse' are partly the outcome of a false education, as he makes clear in *Apropos of Lady Chatterley's Lover:*

'Our education from the start has *taught* us a certain range of emotions, what to feel and what not to feel, and how to feel the feelings we allow ourselves to feel. All the rest is just non-existent. . . . The higher emotions are strictly dead. They have to be faked.'

Lawrence felt the forms of our civilization as an enormous incubus of rottenness and decay—involving a mind-mechanization instead of a living from the 'vital centres'. He felt the contemporary inertness as a great weight upon him, a fact which possibly explains his constant journeyings and his inability to find any resting place; it also explains that blatant assertion which as we have seen, was certainly one of the sides of Lawrence, and which comes out in its absurdity in Aldous Huxley's account of how Lawrence repudiated the scientific notion of evolution: ' "But I don't care about evidence. Evidence doesn't mean anything to me. I don't feel it *here*." And he pressed his two hands on his solar plexus.' The pressure around him was so extreme—the 'horror of little swarming selves'—what, in *Kangaroo*, he calls 'this lit-up cloy of humanity'—that nothing but a tremendous effort of repudiation would have kept his vision

---

[1] As George Orwell says about Dickens: 'Wonderfully as he can describe an appearance Dickens does not often describe a process.' One of Lawrence's great achievements is the conveying of the inner essence of process and movement, in terms of which the external takes on significance; cf. his reply to Edwin Muir's criticism that 'we should not know any of (Lawrence's characters) if we met them in the street'. 'Alas, that I should recognize people in the street, by their noses, bonnets, or beauty. I don't care about their noses, bonnets, or beauty. Does nothing exist beyond that which is recognizable in the street? . . . Ugh, thank God there are more and other sorts of vision than the kodak sort which Mr. Muir esteems above all others.'

clear. What he needed to feel was his own identity in a world which, for all its parade of democratic individuality—because of it—threatens identity.

Nevertheless, the Huxley story, for all the apparent blindness and stupidity it seems to reveal, has its deep significance in the total pattern of Lawrence's morality. It is one of the more astonishing aberrations of criticism that Mr. T. S. Eliot should find in Lawrence an absence of any moral or social sense. To the 'ordinary social morality' which Mr. Eliot accuses Lawrence of lacking Lawrence was not indeed indifferent; he offered a positive repudiation. But to deny him a moral sense altogether can only spring from a considerable misunderstanding of what Lawrence was about, an incompatibility of outlook which has made the two men unable to see each other's point of view. For Lawrence is one of the most profoundly moral writers of his generation. Part of his morality comes, indeed, from the repudiation mentioned above; because he felt the 'ordinary social morality' was so deadly and crippling, led to such 'tortures of psychic starvation', a starvation of the sort he explored in *Women in Love*, for instance.

For Lawrence's morality is the morality of what basically *is*, not the morality of man-made forms. When Newman accepted the Roman Catholic Church, he made it vitally his own; that is to say, he was able to find a fulfilment in what the Church gave him. Newman's acceptance of the Church provides an example of how a man could still fulfil his deepest nature by accepting one of the presented forms of current civilization. Lawrence's genius is of a different sort; partly because he was born at a different time. In the naked honesty of *his* soul, he finds only dross, 'orts, scraps and greasy relics' in the conventionally accepted forms of modern life. Both men fought and hated aspects of the liberal spirit, both ultimately in the cause of their own fundamental integrity. Both have great minds, and both provide a comment on each other. Where they meet, as they do, for Newman's intellectual spirituality has a great deal of controlled emotion in it, and Lawrence's communings with the dark gods takes on a moral and mental aspect, lies in the sphere beyond personality; in what Newman called the Object and what Lawrence termed 'the third ground'.

But I must return to a consideration of Lawrence's morality. It is, as I have said, the morality of what basically *is*. There is an interesting exposition in a letter to Edward Garnett that reveals Lawrence's approach. After objecting to the fixed moral code of the great Russians, he proceeds to discuss Marinetti's (the Italian Futurist's) notion that

'It is the solidity of a blade of steel that is interesting by itself, that is, the incomprehending and inhuman alliance of its molecules in resistance to, let us say, a bullet. The heat of a piece of wood or iron is in fact more passionate, for us, than the laughter or tears of a woman.'

Lawrence calls Marinetti's contrast 'stupid':

'Because what is interesting in the laugh of the woman is the same as the binding of the molecules of steel or their action in heat; it is the inhuman will, call it physiology, or like Marinetti—physiology of matter, that fascinates me. I don't so much care about what the woman *feels*—in the ordinary usage of the word. That presumes an *ego* to feel with. I only care about what the woman *is*—what she is—inhumanly, physiologically, materially —according to the use of the word: but for me, what she *is* as a phenomenon (or as representing some greater inhuman will) instead of what she feels according to the human conception.'[1]

This will receive a fuller exposition later; for the moment, it is interesting to point out that, in this, Lawrence is like Emily Brontë. Just as she is concerned with forces that lie beyond man-made morality, so in a sense is he. The relationship of Heathcliff and Cathy *is*; it searches after no 'fact or reason';[2] and it represents a force beyond themselves, an element of the *in*human: as Cathy says to Nelly Dean,

---

[1] Cf. too, the discussion in *Aaron's Rod* as to why Aaron left his wife. (Chapter XII.)

[2] Cf. Keats's definition of negative capability: '. . . that is, when a man is capable of being in uncertainties, mysteries, doubts, without any irritable reaching after fact and reason. . . .'

'. . . surely you and everybody have a notion that there is or should be an existence of yours beyond you. What were the use of my creation, if I were entirely contained here? . . . If all else perished, and *he* remained *I* should still continue to be . . . My love for Heathcliff resembles the eternal rocks beneath: a source of little visible delight, but necessary. Nelly I *am* Heathcliff.'

Lawrence's morality, I would suggest, is of this order, and must be understood in this sort of context. His work becomes a standard (as Heathcliff and Cathy, in their way, do) by which ordinary conventional human intercourse can be judged; not, incidentally, because he is always 'right', but because the situations exist. Truth to his experience represents neglected forces in mankind, forces perhaps incomplete in themselves (as Cathy found Heathcliff, for, after all, she didn't *marry* him) but essentially *there* at the deepest level and demanding recognition or taking their toll.

But some of this becomes perilously like the mysticism that Lawrence so disliked; we need to look round for a trousers' seat. We find it, oddly enough, situated in that solar plexus that Lawrence pressed in the Huxley story. It is interesting that Lawrence wasn't just content with saying that he didn't believe in evolution; he appealed to an authority: 'I don't feel it *here*,' he said. The solar plexus, indeed, was a most important element in Lawrence's conception of human personality; and to that conception we must now turn, for it is central to Lawrence's educational notions.

In the *Fantasia*, Lawrence draws, briefly, a vital distinction. He speaks of 'My own soul, and myself. Not my ego, my conceit of myself. But my very soul.' It is a distinction we can note in the Garnett letter above. What he means by this becomes plainer when he criticizes the modern spirit, as manifested, in this case, in Bertrand Russell. The quotation is sufficiently central to justify some length:

'I am so sick of people: they preserve an evil, bad, separating spirit under the warm cloak of good words. That is intolerable in them. The conservative talks about the old and glorious national ideal, the Liberal talks about this great struggle for right in which the nation is engaged, the peaceful women talk about disarmament and international peace. Bertie Russell talks about democratic control and the educating of the artisan, and all this, all this goodness, is just a warm and cosy cloak for a bad spirit. They all want the same thing: a continuing in this state of disintegration wherein each separate little ego is an independent little principality by itself. What does Russell really want? He wants to keep his own established ego, his finite and ready-defined self intact, free from contact and connection. He wants to be ultimately a free agent. That is what they all want, ultimately—that is what is at the back of all international peace-for-ever and democratic control talks; they want an outward system of nullity, which they call peace and goodwill, so that in their own souls they can be independent little gods, referred nowhere and to nothing, little mortal Absolutes, secure from question. That is at the back of all Liberalism, Fabianism and democracy.'

From this 'finite and ready defined' self of modern individualism Lawrence turned away completely. For this self was the conscious ego, springing from the mental-spiritual 'mode'; the fixed static will, existing in terms of the 'idea' . . . the idea of democracy or Fabianism or of any other 'ism that happened to be going, or the idea derived from the past and accepted inertly.

'Nothing in the world is more pernicious than the *ego* or spurious self, the conscious entity with which every individual is saddled. He receives it almost *en bloc* from the preceding generation, and spends the rest of his life trying to drag his spontaneous self from beneath the horrible incubus. And the most fatal part of the incubus, by far, is the dead, leaden weight of handed-on ideals.'[1]

It will be noted that there is nothing in this that would, for instance, quarrel with Mr. Eliot's conception of Tradition, already quoted ('Tradition cannot mean standing still'), or with Newman's conception of personality, which needs to make

[1] D. H. Lawrence: *Essay on Democracy.*

a 'real assent' and thus revivify the accepted past; although there is, of course, a certain difference of stress as between Lawrence on the one hand and Newman and Eliot on the other.

Lawrence, then, was here concerned with that part of the personality which produced the abstract and mechanistic elements of modern life, intimately related to that self-consciousness which was strangling modern man to death. For man was living in terms of the 'idea', the abstract notion, of other people, out of the mentally conceived version of himself which modern self-consciousness had permitted him to evolve.[1] The whole effort of Lawrence in his novels was to get below, beneath this conception of the ego, to permit the exploration of a deeper layer of being. In the letter to Garnett, just quoted, he goes on:

'You mustn't look in my novel for the old stable *ego* of the character. There is another *ego*, according to whose action the individual is unrecognizable, and passes through, as it were, allotropic states which it needs a deeper sense than any we've been used to exercise, to discover are states of the same single radically unchanged single element. (Like as diamond and coal are the same pure single element of carbon. The ordinary novel would trace the history of the diamond—but I say, "Diamond, what! This is carbon." And my diamond might be coal or soot, and my theme is carbon.)'

That was apropos of the novel that became *The Rainbow*. What he was trying to get at—what in fact comes out, a little crudely and imperfectly as yet, in *The Rainbow*—was the consciousness that existed below the mental level; the true unconscious, not the Freudian unconscious, that he explores in the *Psychoanalysis and the Unconscious*. This provided a corrective to (*not* necessarily, or always, a repudiation of) the mental conception of the personality . . . 'what the woman is . . . inhumanly, physiologically, materially' rather than what she feels, i.e. what

[1] 'The Freudian unconscious is the cellar in which the mind keeps its own bastard spawn. The true unconscious is the well-head, the fountain of real maturity.'—*Psychoanalysis and the Unconscious*.

she *thinks* she feels. Life lived in terms of the idea[1] or ideal (Lawrence often uses the two words interchangeably) he regards as having strangled the vital, lower centres. His effort is towards a redressing of the balance, to an extent that blinds many people to the fact that he didn't *repudiate* consciousness, and his own life is a tribute to the effort.[2]

It is well known that Lawrence made use of a curious physiological terminology to describe the distinction he wished to make between the mental, spiritual 'centres' and the lower, vital 'centres'. There is no need to follow the details of this terminology; there is no reason to assume that it has any physiological validity. What really matters is the end he had in view in employing it. He was determined that men should again live from the 'vital centres' instead of in terms of their own consciousness of themselves; and this, as we have seen, led him to formulate and repudiate the false individualism of the day: 'The so-called individualism is no more than a cheap egotism, every self-conscious little ego assuming unbounded rights to display his self-consciousness.' Nowadays 'Instead of living from the spontaneous centres we live from the head'; and as a result, 'we have almost poisoned the mass of humanity to death with *understanding*'. It should be emphasized here—more will be said later—that there were a few who must accept mind-consciousness as their goal. But even these must 'know' only to get beyond mind-knowledge, to see the function of the mind as instrument, not as director.

The worst manifestation of the crippling power of mental consciousness was what Lawrence called 'sex in the head', a meeting in terms of an idealization of love instead of a vital coming together. In 'cerebral sex-consciousness' and its depredations and dangers Lawrence finds one of the causes of our

[1] Nowadays, Lawrence pointed out, a girl of eighteen thought she knew what it was to be in love, a deserted wife and a grandmother, because she had arrived at mental conceptions of these experiences. This strikes one as a good example of what Lawrence meant by 'living from the head'.

[2] He even speaks, on one occasion, of the acceptance of his ideas on sex (as he had shown them in *Lady Chatterley's Lover*) as being a 'question of *conscious* acceptance and adjustment'.—*Letters*, p. 773.

emasculated and psychically starved living. His protests against 'sex in the head' provide the clue to his sadly misrepresented notions of sex. His conception of the true significance of sex must be examined with some care. For, after all, sex was obviously deeply involved in what Lawrence saw as the central difficulty of our day. From his immediate personal contacts Lawrence realized the importance of *vital* human relationships —of a sort that our civilization tended to thwart:

'I can only write what I feel pretty strongly about: and that, at present, is the relation between men and women. After all, it is *the* problem to-day, the establishment of a new relation, or the re-adjustment of the old one, between men and women.'

What he writes stems from this.

Ultimately, Lawrence was deeply concerned with the striving that ended beyond personality, in 'divine otherness'. His great contribution to the understanding of the modern world lies in his realization that all the modern 'love' and benevolence of humanitarian democratic notions, being mental in origin, were ultimately only a means to self-inflation, inflation of the ego.[1] And this love idealism, in the final resort, only a form of masturbation, he traced to a wrong conception of sexual relationships between people.

'But there's the trouble; men have most of them got their sex in their heads nowadays, and nowhere else. They start all their deeper reactions in their heads, and work themselves from the top downwards, which, of course, brings disgust, because you're only having yourself all the time, no matter what other individual you take as *machine-à-plaisir*, you're only taking yourself all the time.'

Sex-consciousness involved 'taking oneself' all the time; the humanitarian 'ideal', founded on 'love-consciousness', was basically only a concern for self and one's little ego, in isolation:

'The disease of love, the disease of "spirit", the disease of

[1] Cf. Newman's criticism, p.115.

niceness and benevolence and feeling good on our own behalf and good on somebody else's behalf. Pah, it is all a gangrene.'

And it *was* a gangrene, judged by Lawrence's standards:

'Because, if you think of it, everything which is provoked or originated *by an idea* works automatically or mechanically. It works by principle. . . . No matter which way you *work* the affective centres, once you work them from the mental consciousness you automatize them.'

Anything was better than this mechanization of life—even chaos—'To me, chaos doesn't matter so much as abstract, which is mechanical, order.' So he thought in one of his moods. But actually, as we shall see, what he sought was not chaos, but an infinitely more subtle and delicate order.

What, then, was the way out from the tyranny of the 'upper centres', the automatization of the idea?

'Why don't you *jeunesse* let all the pus of festering sex out of your heads, and try to act from the original centres? The old, dark religions understood. "God enters from below", said the Egyptians, and that's right. Why can't you darken your minds, and know that the great gods pulse in the dark, and enter you as darkness through the lower gates. Not through the head. Why don't you seek again the unknown and invisible gods who step sometimes into your arteries, and down the blood vessels to the phallos, to the vagina, and have strange meetings there? There are different dark gods, different passions. . . . But why don't you leave off your old white festerings in silence, and let a light fall over your mind and heal you? And turn again to the dark gods, which are the dark promptings and passion-motions inside you, and have a reverence for life.'

Now this, as will be seen, involves a very different embodiment in action from the working of the autonomous, self-conscious ego, behaviour in isolation. The religious imagery in which Lawrence couches his descriptions is no accident; he was a deeply religious man, with a reverence before life which so many of his egocentric contemporaries lacked:

'To hear these young people talking really fills me with black fury: they talk endlessly, but endlessly—and never, never a good or real thing said. Their attitude is so irreverent and blatant. They are cased each in a hard little cell of his own, and out of this they talk words. There is never for one second any outgoing of feeling, and no reverence, not a crumb or grain of reverence. I cannot stand it. I *will not* have people like this—I had rather be alone. . . . It is this horror of little swarming selves that I can't stand.'

What he wanted was a flow, an out-going towards people, in the name of something which transcended self and even the other person. Surrender to the dark gods implied a submission to a fundamental religious principle as part of the nature of life, a principle which transcended the pure relationship:

'. . . the human heart must have an absolute. It is one of the conditions of being human. The only thing is the God who is the source of all passion. Once go down before the God-passion and human passions take their right rhythm.'

And again: 'Damn Humanity, let me have a bit of inhuman, or non-human truth, that our human emotions can't alter.'

Thus it is seen that to talk of sex being an ultimate to Lawrence, a matter of obsession, is quite false. Sex, in a sense, was as much an *instrument* to Lawrence as the mind was; though at the moment it needed much more insisting on because so many had conspired to ignore the dark gods which worked through the deep passions. But Lawrence's religious instinct was not satisfied with the *togetherness* of sex. Sexuality, of course, disgusted him: 'Nothing nauseates me more than promiscuous sex in and out of season'; and there was his bitter complaint 'And I, who loathe sexuality so deeply, am considered a lurid sexuality specialist.' What he wanted, what he sought to do, for instance, in *Lady Chatterley's Lover*, was 'to make an *adjustment in consciousness* to the basic realities'; so that people should come together out of the warm glow of themselves, the deep passional embrace, instead of in terms of the *idea* of sex and relationship—

as in the case of the young man who takes the marriage textbook to bed with him on the first night.

'God forbid that I should be taken as urging loose sex activity. There is a brief time for sex, and a long time when sex is out of place. But when it is out of place as an activity there still should be the large and quiet space in the consciousness where it lives quiescent.'

For the religious consciousness in Lawrence manifested itself in other modes than in the immediacies of sexual relationship. And now we begin to approach the 'rooted' Lawrence. The breaking free, the sheer assertion was necessary as a preliminary to the 'adjustment in consciousness'; but, inside the assertion, informing it as a spirit and turning it into something beyond itself, is the desire for 'connection' and reverence, the tribute to the eternal *other* in the universe. The God-passion must be served, as a means to the right anchoring of the human psyche in true centrality.

We get the clue to this other and yet vitally connected side of Lawrence in his realization of himself as artist, as *impersonal* maker, that is.

'One needs something to make one's mood deep and sincere. There are so many little frets that prevent our coming at the real naked essence of our vision. It sounds boshy, doesn't it? I often think one ought to be able to pray, before one works—and then leave it to the Lord. Isn't it hard, hard work to come to real grips with one's imagination—throw everything overboard. I always feel as if I stood naked for the fire of Almighty God to go through me—and it's rather an awful feeling. One has to be so terribly religious, to be an artist.'

And again, once when he was rebuked by Edward Garnett, he felt the chastisement as an insult not to himself but to the 'thing I *wanted* to say, and had failed in'; the careful distinction is worth noting. 'But primarily I am a passionately religious man, and my novels must be written from the depth of my religious experience.'

This truth then, to the 'religious, earnest, suffering man in me' provides a Lawrence who is faithful to the religious 'given' part of himself and provides him with the purpose which exists beyond relationship. 'I believe that the highest virtue is to be happy, living in the greatest truth, not submitting to *the false-hood of these personal times*.'[1] If there was a part of Lawrence which sought fulfilment in pure relationship, with his mother, with his wife and spasmodically, through his dreamed Utopia of Rananim, in pure community, there was another Lawrence who sought his deep satisfaction through 'the greatest truth', in his own ultimate aloneness and peace in the impersonal universe, rooted and secure.[2]

This side of Lawrence, which has received less attention than it should, explains his use of the phrase 'falsehood of these personal times'. Something of what he meant should have emerged from the consideration above of the false individualism he condemned. But it is time to see the effect of this repudiation on his positive conception, something gouged out of the 'religious, earnest, suffering man'.

Middleton Murry, in his autobiography, has pointed out how insistent was Lawrence's distaste for the "personal", as he understood that word. The time came when the bond of Rananim was to be "impersonal; it was to be soldered by the melting-down of personality in surrender to some great and all-inclusive religious purpose." What Lawrence wanted was a

---

[1] My italics.

[2] This makes nonsense of this comment, made by Mr. Anthony West in his recent study of Lawrence: 'Lawrence was one of those people with a rich emotional life who became emotional topers. He found friendship an inadequate relationship; he had to go beyond it, to become a lover, to possess the whole mind.' That this was potentially Lawrence is true. There was his all-absorbing relationship with his mother. Murry, rightly or wrongly, noted his desire for absorption in his wife; and on the other side—the desire for possession—there is the evidence of the poem 'The Best of School' quoted above and at times, perhaps, the persistent efforts after Rananim. But these stages of development do not justify calling Lawrence an emotional toper. The whole point about Lawrence was that he went beyond this sort of thing, and *saw it for what it was*. His rejection of Middleton Murry shows his later rejection of any form of love parasitism: 'Cut all that would-be sympathetic stuff out.'

" 'unity in religious belief, which leads to action'. We were to be centred 'in the knowledge of the Infinite, of God', and work from that centre".'[1]

In a letter at that period to Katherine Mansfield, Lawrence defines his purpose:

'One thing I know, I am tired of this insistence on the *personal* element; personal truth, personal reality. It is very stale and profitless. I want some new non-personal activity which is at the same time a genuine vital activity. And I want relations which are not purely personal, based on purely personal qualities; but relations based on some unanimous accord in truth or belief, and a harmony of *purpose*, rather than of personality. I am weary of personality. It remains now whether Murry is still based upon the personal hypothesis: because if he is, then our ways are different. I don't want a purely personal relation with him: he is a man, therefore our relation should be based on *purpose*; not upon that which we *are*, but upon that which we wish to bring to pass. I am sick and tired of personality in every way. Let us be easy and impersonal, not for ever fingering over our own souls, and the souls of our acquaintances, but trying to create a new life, a new common life, a new complete tree of life from the roots that are within us. I am weary to death of these dead, dry leaves of personalities which flap in every wind. . . . We must grow from our deepest underground roots, out of the *unconsciousness*, not from the conscious concepts that we falsely call ourselves.'

Here, then, in the repudiation of 'personality', the dark gods and the non-personal activity meet. Out of the deep religious personality must come at once sex-passion and purpose; and the rhythm of relationship in sex must take its meaning and significance from what lies beyond sex. Sex, as everyone has recognized, was very important to Lawrence; but once more it must be insisted that it was *not* ultimate. And the clue perhaps comes in the sentence 'I want some new non-personal activity which is at the same time a genuine vital activity'; only if the

[1] Middleton Murry: *Between Two Worlds.*

dark gods held their sway, *through* non-cerebral sexual activity, could the individual be said to live again from the 'vital centres'; but when the individual so lived, his *aim* was not sex, but that which lay over beyond sex, in non-personal activity, '. . . individuals do not *vitally* concern me any more. Only a *purpose* vitality concerns me, not individuals—neither my own individual self, nor any other'. To accept other people as the standard was, in the last resort, to accept oneself as the ultimate:

'Is there nothing beyond my fellow man? If not, then there is nothing beyond myself, beyond my own throat, which may be cut, and my own purse, which may be slit: because *I* am the fellow-man of all the world, my neighbour is but myself in a mirror. So we toil in a circle of pure egoism.'

Like Newman, Lawrence reveals the profound egocentricity of the modern world—an egocentricity which is all the more dangerous for being hidden, cloaked under an appearance of altruism.

All this is made explicit in that wonderful diagnosis of our present wants and inadequacies, *Fantasia of the Unconscious*. The *Fantasia*, as Lawrence makes clear in his Foreword, emerges from the experience of the artist, a quintessence of the life-knowledge distilled from the novels. 'I proceed by intuition', he states; but because his are the intuitions of a great artist, they tell us infinitely more about the human psyche and the human mind than the abstractions of the 'scientific educators'. It is odd, indeed, how little educationalists have used the insight provided by artists and writers in their formulation of their educational 'theories'.[1] What, in fact, is needed in education is not the 'mind-knowledge', to use Lawrence's phrase, of the social scientist, but the insight and 'intuition' to which one can be

[1] '. . . being a novelist, I consider myself superior to the saint, the scientist, the philosopher and the poet, who are all great masters of different bits of man alive, but never get the whole hog. The novel is the one bright book of life. Books are not life. They are only tremulations on the ether. But the novel as a tremulation can make the whole man alive tremble, which is more than poetry, philosophy, science, or any other book-tremulation can do.' (*Why the Novel Matters*)

helped by the profound understanding of the great artist; 'intuition' of course, controlled by the integrity of the artist, not any and every gleam of the 'inner light'. Because the great novels of Lawrence are so sure and profound, one can trust these 'pollyanalytics', as he calls them:

'This pseudo-philosophy of mine—"pollyanalytics", as one of my respected critics might say—is deduced from the novels and poems, not the reverse. The novels and poems come unwatched out of one's pen. And then the absolute need that one has for some sort of satisfactory mental attitude towards oneself and things in general makes one try to abstract some definite conclusions from one's experiences as a writer and as a man. The novels and poems are pure passionate experience. These "pollyanalytics" are inferences made afterwards, from the experience.'

Fantasia, then, is implicit in the relationships of Lawrence's characters, in the working out, below the conscious ego (as he himself made clear), of the attractions and antagonisms that go to make up the fundamental human urges; the book exposes those 'conscious' conclusions for the human situation which Lawrence drew from his insight. His 'pollyanalytics' give powerful support to his criticisms in his letters of these 'personal times'. Here is the quintessence of his vision:

'With sex as the one accepted prime motive, the world drifts into despair and anarchy. . . . Sex holds any *two* people together, but it tends to disintegrate society, unless it is subordinated to the great dominating male passion of collective purpose.'

And here one gets the final statement of the relation of the two aspects of man, the sexual, and the purposive, basically religious, inhuman sides:

'Assert sex as the predominant fulfilment, and you get the collapse of living purpose in man. You get anarchy. Assert *purposiveness* as the one supreme and pure activity of life, and you drift into barren sterility, like our business life of to-day, and our political life. You become sterile, you make anarchy inevitable. And so there you are. You have got to base your great purpos-

ive activity upon the intense sexual fulfilment of all your individuals. But you have got to keep your sexual fulfilment even
then subordinate, just subordinate to the great passion of purpose; subordinate by a hair's breadth only: but still, by that
hair's breadth, subordinate.'

So there are, then, two ways of fulfilment:

'The first, the way of fulfilment through complete love, complete, passionate, deep love. And the second, the greater, the
fulfiment through the accomplishment of religious purpose, the
soul's earnest purpose.'

To make love-idealism the end, as our civilization, in its
various guises, attempts to do, is to invite disaster.

The deep psychic fulfilment of marriage and what it implies
in the most secret places is the great theme of *Women in Love*.
Ursula and Birkin seek their way to a relationship in something
that exists beyond relationship. Gerald and Gudrun both fail
in their differing ways because they seek their fulfilment in 'love'
only. There is a conversation between Ursula and Gudrun that
points the way: Gudrun is speaking . . .

' "You above everybody can't get away from the fact that
love is the supreme thing, in space as well as on earth."

' "No," said Ursula, "it isn't. Love is too human and little.
I believe in something of which love is only a little part. I
believe what we must fulfil comes out of the unknown to us, and
is something infinitely more than love. It isn't so merely *human*."

'Gudrun looked at Ursula with steady, balancing eyes. She
admired and despised her sister so much, both! Then, suddenly
she averted her face, saying coldly, uglily:

' "Well, I've got no further than love, yet."

'Over Ursula's mind flashed the thought: "Because you never
have loved, you can't get beyond it." '

Both Gerald and Gudrun exist in the *will*; this is partly the
reason for their seeking their consummation in 'love'. After the
death of his father, Gerald arrives (largely because his sense of
'purpose' is awry) at a dependence on Gudrun which she comes

to hate and reject. Her 'critical consciousness', having once 'known' Gerald, and existing only in the 'subtle thrills of extreme sensation in reduction', needs to go on beyond him:

'. . . between two people, any two people on earth, the range of pure sensational experience is limited. The climax of sensual reaction, once reached in any direction, is reached finally, there is no going on.'

Gerald can offer to her only the experience of the world. 'In him she knew the world, and had done with it.' And so Loerke takes his place, for 'He, Loerke, could penetrate into depths far out of Gerald's knowledge'. Thus those who exist only in terms of the mind-knowledge of the world, the automatisms of the will (which is what Gerald is made to represent in the book), with its underlying cynicism and sensuality, are lost, as Gerald is lost. His motion is a swaying from the mechanistic demands of pure will and the idealizations of social life to the utter dependence of sensuality masquerading as love. He has no 'purpose' beyond 'will' and 'love'; 'to have no claim upon her, he must stand by himself, in sheer nothingness.' And so he remains a symbol of the tragedy of the modern world:

'Sex as an end in itself is a disaster: a vice. But an ideal purpose which has no roots in the deep sea of passionate sex is a greater disaster still. And now we have only these two things: sex as a fatal goal, which is the essential theme of modern tragedy: or ideal purpose as a deadly parasite.'[1]

Gerald Crich as industrial magnate and as lover combines the two disasters in his own person.

So by now some conception of what Lawrence meant by right relationship should be coming clearer:

[1] An example of the deadly effect of idealization in love comes to mind in the person of Charles Dickens. Dickens was incapable of real relationship —and his incapability is reflected in his moods. His ego created ideal pictures for him of those who were unattainable, like Mary Hogarth—selfish projections of his own *idea* of what he wanted in the other person. Hence he is for ever fascinated by 'appearances' with which most of his writing is concerned.

'One needs to establish a fuller relationship between oneself and the universe, and between oneself and one's fellow men and fellow women. It doesn't mean cutting out the "brothers-in-Christ" business simply: it means expanding it into a full relationship, where there can be also physical and passional meeting, as there used to be in the old dances and rituals. We have to know how to go out to meet one another, upon the third ground, the holy ground . . . We need to come forth and meet in the essential physical self, on some third holy ground.'

Both the connected and the 'proud isolate' self play a part in it. The rootedness is religious in essence: 'But one has to drive one's peg down to the centre of the earth: or one's root: it's the same thing'; for 'I do think that man is related to the universe in some religious way, even prior to his relation to his fellow man'. Firmly rooted in purpose and the coming together of deep passional embrace in tribute to the dark gods, one needed also to be able to swing back into the 'centre of sensual, manly independence, of exultation in the sturdy defiant self, wilfulness and masterfulness and pride'. Lawrence's persistence in evoking 'manly pride' is very marked. Part of it springs from this desire to thrust away the awful clingingness of modern abstract desires, desires from the 'upper centres', the 'slime of all the world's my friend, my half-friend, anyway I'm not going to make an enemy of him'. When he proclaims 'God in me is my desire', he is not making the egotistical statement he seems to be doing. For he is not referring to the thought-wishes, the 'ideas' of desire stimulated from the upper centres, but the deep passional desires that lead a man to the centre of his being, in self-understanding,[1] and out again to the external world. 'I shall find my deepest desire to be a wish for pure unadulterated relationship

[1] Part of the proof of Lawrence's insight comes from the soundness of the advice he gave in concrete situations: his analysis of the relationship between Murry and Katherine Mansfield is a case in point: 'She must see if she really *wants* you, wants to keep you and to have no other man all her life. It means forfeiting something. But the only principle I can see in this life is that one *must* forfeit the less for the greater. Only one must be thoroughly honest about it.' He reveals the basic egotism of Murry's unselfishness in not living on Katherine Mansfield's money.

with the universe, for truth in being.' He was protesting against the abstract 'caring' that consumes the modern mind to the exclusion of all deep real being; so that abstract principles consume people, instead of people being able to live their principle:

'They are simply eaten up with caring. They are so busy caring about Fascism or Leagues of Nations or whether France is right or whether Marriage is threatened, that they never know where they are. They certainly never live on the spot where they are. They inhabit abstract space, the desert void of politics, principles, right and wrong, and so forth. They are doomed to be abstract. Talking to them is like trying to have a human relationship with the letter x in algebra.[1]

Paradoxically, Lawrence's 'desire' hides a deep humility; it permitted an out-flowing to the external world, whereas the apparent humbleness of the modern self-conscious individual conceals a basic arrogance because all experience is referred to that static idea of the self, the 'persona', to use the language of modern psychology, in terms of which he lives and behaves. No one knew this better than Lawrence, in full vivid concrete immediacy; his wonderful capacity to evoke the spirit of place, whether it be the filth of industrial England or the mysteriousness of the Australian bush, is sufficient indication of his capacity for an out-flowing to what is about him. In that respect, he is the least self-conscious of modern writers. And the wish that all should share his capacity for personal individual response—what one *sees*, not what one thinks one sees—a capacity which is the supreme gift of Lawrence, and which produced the great novels, lies behind his consistent emphasis on the necessity of human isolation and pride. The characters in Lawrence's novels are constantly evoked as proud, unbending, regal; when Mrs. Morel teaches young Paul how to blanch almonds, she does it 'feeling queenly'. Behind these apparently disproportionate epithets lies Lawrence's intense feeling of the ultimate dignity of human beings, when they are being themselves; so that the most commonplace actions and the drabbest of people

[1] 'Insouciance', reprinted in *Assorted Articles*.

acquire an immense richness, and the most trivial of events an importance in accordance with the vitality of human desires and the genuineness of human 'being', rather than the abstract 'importance' in the fixed moral scheme, that enters into them. And it was an essential part of this human dignity that it should be able to rest in isolation, in the possession of its own soul. 'We've got to learn to live from the centre of our own responsibility only, and let other people do the same.' And again

'Till a man makes the great resolution of aloneness and singleness of being, till he takes upon himself the silence and central appeasedness of maturity; and *then, after this*, assumes a sacred responsibility for the next purposive step into the future, there is no rest. The great resolution of aloneness and appeasedness and the further deep assumption of responsibility in purpose— this is necessary to every parent, every father, every husband, at a certain point. If the resolution is never made, the responsibility never embraced, then the love-craving will run on into frenzy, and lay waste to the family.'

This notion of 'proud isolate self' then, is not absolute. It involves an acceptance within the self of one's own fullness of being, so as not to be smeared with the 'Judas-Jesus slime'; but the purpose lies in the ultimate giving forth, from out of this deep inviolable self; in the words of some further advice to Middleton Murry: 'Can't you focus yourself outside yourself? Not for ever focused on yourself, *ad nauseam.*' For what we must do is to get away from the modern possessiveness, the finding of satisfaction, not in the deep self, but in the 'fingering over' of other people:

'We must depend on the wholeness of our being, ultimately only on that, which is our Holy Ghost within us. Whereas in an ideal of love and benevolence, we have tried to automatize ourselves into little love engines always stoked with the sorrows and beauties of other people, so that we can get up steam of charity or righteous wrath.'

The paradox is, that the love-benevolence idealism is ultimately based on selfishness, a desire to find our fulfilment and our self-esteem, not through ourselves, not what we ultimately *are* in connection with the great *impersonal* forces of the universe, but through our parasitic, blood-sucking life on the emotions of others. We need to give something else besides interference and 'caring'. As Birkin, in *Women in Love*, puts it:

'I want every man to have his share in the world's goods, so that I am rid of his importunity, so that I can tell him: "Now you've got what you want—you've got your fair share of the world's gear. Now, you one-mouthed fool, mind yourself and don't obstruct me." '

There is more altruism, more real social morality, in Birkin's repudiation, more ultimate respect for humanity, than there is in much of the apparent self-immolation of the social worker. But how few, except Lawrence, have dared to say so.

So it is here, then, that the two Lawrences meet—the rooted Lawrence and the Lawrence of the isolate self; they are not contradictory aspects of the same personality, but complementary. The one needs the other for any sort of completeness, just as the real deep love needs hate for its fulfilment; so that in the ensuing battle, once 'we have come through',[1] there will be 'peace and inner security, no matter how many things go wrong'. And then there is completeness of being on both sides:

'Because really, being alone in peace means being two people together. Two people who can be silent together, and not conscious of one another outwardly. Me in my silence, she in hers, and the balance, the equilibrium, the pure circuit between us.'

It remains to examine the effect of these ideas, which form the centre from which Lawrence spoke his criticisms of modern life, and which give these criticisms their validity. It was because Lawrence, for all his restlessness and the deficiency of his 'societal instinct', achieved something of the peace of inner, deep being that what he has to say on contemporary society

[1] Taken from the title, 'Look we have come through', of a series of poems in which Lawrence describes his relationship with his wife.

has such immense value. He never compromised; he was never parasitic: 'Learn that I am not lovable: hence not betrayable,' he wrote to Middleton Murry. His comments come out of a 'religious, earnest, suffering man', refusing to be 'pawed and bullied'.

Naturally, then, he repudiated 'that weird and horrible animal, Social Man'. He repudiated, too, what mental consciousness was producing in those lower classes which still retained something of their pre-mental warmth of the 'old England', when 'the curious blood-connection held the classes together. The squire might be arrogant, violent, bullying and unjust, yet in some ways they were *at one* with the people, part of the same blood-stream.' The miners of his home neighbourhood, 'passionate enough, sensuous, dark—God, how all my boyhood comes back—so violent, so dark, the mind always dark and without understanding, the senses violently active', these men, once they come to understand, '*understand* mentally so horribly: only industrialism, only wages and money and machinery. They can't *think* anything else . . . they are utterly unable to appreciate any pure, ulterior truth: only this industrial—mechanical—wage idea.' And so

'That is why we are *bound* to get something like Guild-Socialism in the long run, which is a reduction to the lowest terms—nothing higher than that which now is, only lower. . . . It is necessary to get the germ of a new development *towards the highest*, not a reduction to the lowest.'

So he demanded a revolution, 'not to install soviets, but to give life itself a chance. What's the good of an industrial system piling up rubbish, while nobody lives.' The chosen solution was *not* the welfare state: 'The dead materialism of Marx socialism and soviets seems to me no better than what we've got.' The old living warmth of the miner's life was better than anything that the false hypocritical idealistic loving-kindness of a Thomas Crich could provide, or that the 'rationalized' methods of production which his son employed could produce: for both ultimately insulted the manhood of the miners. In the long run, even 'twelve hours' work a day is better than a newspaper at four in the afternoon and a grievance for the rest of the evening'. Had Lawrence lived, he might have added: 'Better illiteracy than semi-literate *New Statesmen* men and women'; for as he saw,

'Our leaders have not loved men: they have loved ideas, and have been willing to sacrifice passionate men on the altars of the blood-drinking, ever-ash-thirsty ideal. Has President Wilson, or Karl Marx or Bernard Shaw[1] ever felt one hot blood-pulse of love for the working man, the half-conscious, deluded working man? Never. Each of these leaders has wanted to abstract him away from his own blood and being into some foul Methuselah or abstraction of a man.'

Many men, indeed the majority, should never be brought to self-consciousness, should never be asked to accept the responsibility of the vote:

'Let us have done with this foolish form of government, and this idea of democratic control. Let us submit to the knowledge that there are aristocrats and plebians born, not made. Some amongst us are born fit to govern, and some are born only fit to be governed. Some are born to be artisans and labourers, some to be lords and governors.'

Into the notion of equality Lawrence brought two criteria. Men were at once (or should be) spontaneously themselves and therefore incomparable: 'One man isn't any better than any other, not because they are equal, but because they are intrinsically *other*, that there is no term of comparison', as Birkin points out. And yet, as in the practical world comparison is inevitable, men are immediately seen to be unequal; it is a fact of experience and undeniable. Therefore, the preaching of the idea of equality, instead of being a means of freedom, genuine freedom, to man, produces the distortions inevitable in any living from the *idea*. What, indeed, is the result: 'Your man is no longer a man, living his own life from his own spontaneous centres. He is a theoretic imbecile trying to frustrate and dislocate all life.'

[1] How this is born out by Miss Blanche Patch's revelations!

159

To force people into the mould of theoretic democracy seemed to Lawrence a distortion, a placing of responsibility on every individual which the vast majority were totally incapable of bearing; he saw the paradox that democracy thwarted true individuality by foisting on all and sundry a theoretic individuality. It is in the ultimate interests of the working man that Lawrence cries:

'I would like him to give me back the responsibility for general affairs, a responsibility which he can't acquit, and which saps his life. . . .

'I would like him to give me back books and newspapers and theories. And I would like to give him back, in return, his old insouciance, and rich, original spontaneity and fullness of life.'

As I pointed out earlier—and the time has now come to clear up the apparent discrepancy—there *were* some who had to accept mind-knowledge as their lot. It is a mistake to regard Lawrence as submitting all to the same regimen, or as being an enemy of the mind—in its proper place. He didn't want that reversion to the savage state which many of his detractors (and admirers) have made out for him. *St. Mawr* alone should prove that—in Lou's rejection of Phoenix, and explicitly in 'For all savagery is half-sordid. And man is only himself when he is fighting on and on, to overcome the savagery.' And again, in the *Fantasia*, 'The savage in a state of nature is one of the most conventional of creatures'.

It was the automatizations of democratic convention that Lawrence found so crippling. If the aim was the type of individuality we have discussed, every individual coming to the fulfilment of himself, then 'Mental consciousness is a purely individual affair. Some men are born to be highly and delicately conscious.' It is for the majority that 'much mental consciousness is simply a catastrophe, a blight'; for them 'knowledge *must* be symbolical, mythical, dynamic'. Yet this depended on a 'higher, responsible, conscious class', who should see that all symbols are 'true from top to bottom'. Again and again he insists, 'there are a *few, few* people in whom the living impulse

and reaction develops and sublimates into mental consciousness'. But they exist; and they are the leaders:

'The secret is, to commit into the hands of the sacred few the
responsibility which now lies like torture on the mass. Let the
few, the leaders, be increasingly responsible for the whole. And
let the mass be free: free, save for the choice of leaders.'

But they are to be leaders 'for life's sake only'; and one has to
bear in mind the full richness with which Lawrence invested
the 'man alive'. Only when some such order has come
about would men 'possess their own souls in natural pride'.
Those who are to know are thus to put knowledge in its true
place in the living activity of man, 'And we must know deeply,
in order even to do that'.

In the choice of leaders, there is to be no automatism; it will
be the business of educators—the priests of life—'to estimate the
profound life quality, the very nature of the child, that which
makes him ultimately what he is', so as to judge his capacities
and rank . . . the ultimate 'living understanding—not intellectual
understanding', which belongs merely to the technical activities.
It is obvious that Lawrence's conception of 'living understanding' bears a considerable relationship to Newman's 'illumination' or 'philosophy'. Such an approach will make the system
'primarily religious, and only secondarily practical. Our supreme judges and our master professors will be primarily
priests', because they will have behind them the almost esoteric
'like-knowledge' that Lawrence so desiderates.

And so Lawrence's vision of the true democracy is of one
where

'a people gradually cumulate, from the vast base of the populace upwards through the zones of life and understanding to the
summit where the great man, or the most perfect utterer, is
alone';

instead of the false democracy, where 'every issue, even the
highest, is dragged down to the lowest issue . . . to-day, the
wage'. What it comes to is what he has to say in the last lines
of the *Fantasia*: 'Better passion and death than any more of

these "isms"!' Another way of putting it appears in a letter: 'Don't think of me as a raving, impractical, vain individual. To be material at this juncture is hopeless, hopeless—or worse than impractical.'[1]

[II]

Now, what, it may well already have been asked, has all this to do with Lawrence's specific educational views, with which this essay is ostensibly concerned. The answer, of course, is—everything. Lawrence's educational views are not isolated from the rest of his 'pollyanalytics'; they form an integral part of them; they grow out of that view of life embedded in the rest of his work and letters. So, indeed, they should.[2] We cannot talk about our ideas on education in isolation; for, as I have urged, the sorts of things we say about education will, consciously or unconsciously, bear witness to our views on the nature of man, to our fundamental convictions about the 'man alive'. Before we can have anything valid to say about education, we need to have probed the psychic depths, and to have come to our own conclusions about the fundamental values of our civilization and their worth. That is why—it is necessary to insist once more—the artists are so much better guides than the professional educators; because the artist's vision of life is at

[1] One way of demonstrating that Lawrence was no 'raving, impractical, vain individual' would be to cite the astonishing sureness and felicity of his judgements of people, which showed how profound was his grasp of the essential person. There is his comment on Bertrand Russell: 'What ails Russell is in matter of life and emotion, the inexperience of youth. He is, vitally and emotionally, much too inexperienced in personal contact and conflict, for a man of his age and calibre'—a view borne out by the comparative poverty of Russell's social writings. Again, there is the admirable account of his relationship with Middleton Murry, where he exposes the insincerities of the lesser man: 'And the me that you say you love is not me, but an idol of your own imagination. Believe me, you don't love me. The animal that I am you instinctively dislike . . . we don't know one another—if you knew *how* little we know one another.' Cf. too, his admirable analysis of the 'delicate friendship' business, in his letter to Dorothy Brett.

[2] 'It is useless to think that we can get along without a conception of what man is, and without a belief in ourselves, and without the morality to support this belief.' (*Education of the People*)

once profounder and more subtly concrete than the educator's. The artist, when he bothers about education, can see it in a context, in relation to the rest of human existence, of which his understanding is profounder, in terms of 'life-knowledge', than that of the ordinary man. Moreover, the sensitivities of the artist are of much greater use in education than the abstractions of the psychologists. The range of awareness and understanding of the network of relationship that Lawrence shows, for instance, in the chapter in *Kangaroo* about the meeting of Jack, Victoria, Harriet and Somers, the subconscious half-awareness, the subtleties that no psychologist could give, reveal intensely aspects of group life with which after all the educationist is very much concerned. The danger with the psychologist's theory is that it tends to be applied as a formula. No one would be tempted to *apply* Lawrence's understanding—the range of one's awareness would simply be extended. What, too, Lawrence possesses and what many psychologists lack is a firm sense of values; so that the 'discovery' about human nature is related always to a firmly grasped, concrete understanding of life which can relate significant detail to ultimate purpose. Obviously there is no omniscience; but we accept the behaviour patterns of Lawrence's characters because we feel that what these patterns reveal is firmly and coherently apprehended. Psychologists tend to think in terms of the 'idea' of the action or motivation; like all scientists they must abstract and generalize; their 'patterns of behaviour' are abstractions; the total configuration inevitably escapes the grasp.

And yet such contentions are likely to set up some resistance in the minds of professional educators, secure in their abstract dabblings in psychology and sociology. Lawrence himself knew the oppositions of minds of a comprehension less than his own: 'They all seem determined to make a freak of me—to save their own short-failings, and make them "normal".' The self-protective devices of the human ego are infinite; it needs the 'nakedness for the fire of Almighty God to go through' a Lawrence and the 'hard, hard work' that entails before the essence of the vision is revealed. But when it is, we feel the rightness of

Lawrence's faith in himself: 'I think, do you know, I have inside me a sort of answer to the *want* of to-day: to the real deep want of the English people, not to just what they fancy they want.'

This appreciation of the *deep* want, this profound exploration of the human psyche and its fundamental drives and purposes, which Lawrence accomplished as profoundly as any other person of our generation—equalled, as complement, only perhaps by Mr. Eliot—makes his remarks on education more worth listening to than those of any other writer in England in the last half-century. Lawrence's suggestions emerge from the fullness of his vision of the wants. If we want to teach children how to live, it is vital that the conception of living shall be a high and valid one; and it is vital that our understanding of the children themselves shall be similarly acceptable. The apparent strangeness of Lawrence's ideas is only strange to those who won't face *themselves*. There is no need to agree with everything he says; but it is essential to realize that he matters.

Lawrence's recommendations, then, spring from that view of the nature of human existence which I have attempted to expound in the first part of this essay, and can only be appreciated in relation to it. When, therefore, he says that the goal of education is that 'Every individual is to be helped, wisely, reverently, towards his own natural fulfilment' or 'Every man shall be himself, shall have every opportunity to come to his own intrinsic fullness of being' or 'The final aim is not to *know* but *to be*', we need to understand each word in his exposition in terms of those notions of 'being' and 'individuality' which I have developed above, and which give what otherwise might well seem merely emotive, commonplace phrases their intense validity and worth. Many of these words and phrases supply the commonplaces of present-day educational exposition . . . but as we shall see, Lawrence supplies an infinitely richer meaning. 'Fullness of being' must be read with all Lawrence at the back of it . . . novels, letters, 'pollyanalytics'; not that everyone can be a Lawrence, but that everyone can achieve, *at his own level*, the richness of living that Lawrence wanted for him. What is fundamental is that individuality in *rootedness* which marks the transcendence and reconciliation of those opposites with which I opened this essay.

'The highest goal for every man is the goal of pure individual being. But it is a goal you cannot reach by the mere rupture of all ties. A child isn't born by being torn from the womb. When it is born by natural process that is rupture enough. But even then the ties are not broken. They are only subtilized.'

Now all this goes to explain some of the apparent discrepancies in Lawrence's exposition. It explains the supreme paradox which lies at the back of all this teaching on education:

'So let our ideal be living, spontaneous individuality in every man and woman. Which living spontaneous individuality, being the hardest thing of all to come at, will need the most careful rearing.'

Here then, we have the quintessence of Lawrence's creed; and we must examine it closely to clarify the seeming contradiction.

It will be clear from what has been said above that Lawrence profoundly despised the current creed of egotistic individuality; this contempt he carries over in to his recommendations on the right method of educating children; and he links it here, as elsewhere, with his rejection of the automatization of the *idea*, which is also vitally relevant.

In education, the tyranny of the idea can exercise a doubly crippling effect; it can pervert the educator and it can thwart the true nature of the child. It is therefore doubly to be avoided. Thus Lawrence rejects the self-expressive school of educational thought because such self-conscious expression of self is corrupting both to teacher and taught. 'Nothing is so subject to small, but fatal automatization as a child'; none more deeply conventional. Education, however, 'is supposed to be a process of learning to escape the automatism of ideas, to live direct from the spontaneous, vital centre of oneself'. But paradoxically, this spontaneity has to be *learned*; one has to come to a knowledge of the deep self by 'hard, hard work' . . . Lawrence's own experience as a writer. The deep, 'spontaneous' self of the novels involves a transcendence, not a regression;[1] it is analogous to Wordsworth's 'spontaneous overflow', with the 'long and deep thought' that went into it, which has already been mentioned in Chapter Three when some of the ambiguities of the conception were examined. 'Man is never spontaneous, as we imagine the thrushes or the sparrow hawk, for example, to be spontaneous.' And again:

'Nowadays we like to talk about spontaneity, spontaneous feeling, spontaneous passion, spontaneous emotion. But our very spontaneity is just an idea. All our modern spontaneity is fathered in the mind, gestated in self-consciousness.'

Nevertheless, Lawrence considers it is possible to approach a sort of spontaneousness which transcends the automatization of ideal mind-consciousness, a spontaneity which responds to the immediate situation from the deep being, not in terms of the inert mind-idea,[2] one which arises either through a transcendence of the tyranny of the 'idea' or an avoidance of any such

---

[1] This, I think, explains the paradox of those who complain that no one had 'sex in the head' more than Lawrence himself. The complaint is true to the extent that Lawrence had to express his views on sex as 'ideas'; it is false because the 'ideas' about sex he was expressing were something very different from the sort of 'sex in the head' he was condemning in others. He was not, that is to say guilty of anything like the same 'sex in the head' as those who accuse him of it like to pretend; and he is capable of criticizing his own 'ideas'. Birkin, in *Women in Love*, is partly a projection of Lawrence; but he is not co-extensive with Lawrence. He is a means through which Lawrence tests, in the concrete, those 'ideas'—about sex among other things—he has himself arrived at. Thus Hermione, on the question of self-consciousness in children, explicitly parodies the Lawrentian doctrine. (Cf. F. R. Leavis: *Women in Love* (II). *Scrutiny*, March 1951.) And thus Lawrence shows himself capable of self-criticism as he explores layer beneath layer of consciousness. This, too, I think protects Lawrence from his critics.

[2] Thus Lawrence speaks of 'Pure morality (as) an instinctive adjustment which the soul makes in every circumstance, adjusting one thing to another, livingly, delicately, sensitively. There can be no law.' What, it will be asked, is the difference between this and Dewey's 'education must be conceived as a continuing reconstruction of experience'. The answer is to be found in the difference between a Dewey and a Lawrence, and the 'idea' of human personality which lies behind the two writers' work. Dewey's con-

compulsion-motif of the sort which our rationally conscious civilization has so mistakenly, in Lawrence's view, made obligatory for all.

This, then, I take to be the centre of Lawrence's educational efforts . . . 'spontaneity' defined in the sort of way I have attempted to define it, a care for the immediate situation but the *deep being* going into it and seeing it as something beyond the immediate. All else follows from this central position . . . views on self-expression, adult-child relationship, who shall be educated, discipline and curriculum. That some of these views will be found to be wildly impracticable, that the old accusations, applied to Lawrence, that 'there is no such animal' will be indignantly revived, is no reason for not examining where Lawrence's insight leads him.

'We talk about individuality, and try to drag up every weed into a rose bush.'

Part of Lawrence's criticism of the notion of self-expression is contained in this sentence. For indeed, at the bottom of all the talk of self-expression, there is, as Lawrence noted, an ambiguity. Firstly, 'which self was left vague: a child was to be given a lump of soft clay and told to express himself, presumably in the pious hope that he might model a Tanagra figure or a Donatello plaque, all on his lonely-o.' Implicit, then, in the notion of self-expression is the desire of the educator that only a certain one of the possible selves shall be expressed:

'Now it is obvious that every boy's first act of self-expression would be to throw the lump of soft clay at something: preferably the teacher. This impulse is to be suppressed. On what grounds, metaphysically? since the soft clay was given for self-expression. To this just question there is no answer.'

ception, as it appears in his work, is just one of those automatic mind-ideas that Lawrence condemns. Lawrence's 'idea' is a semi-poetic expression of a delicately exploratory kind which when responded to in the right sort of way, enlarges the awareness and consciousness instead of supplying a formula to be applied in the inert manner that Deweyism, for all its *appearance* of freedom, too frequently encourages.

There are occasions, with certain selected natures, when one could agree with Lawrence when he says:

'Is not radical *unlearnedness* just as true a form of self-expression and just as desirable a state, for many natures (even the bulk) as learnedness?'

It is because we start with the abstract idea of the self of people, because we have a notion in our minds of what *all* people ought to become,[1] and because we are pushed to that notion by the falseness of our democratic position ('disinterested nobility of heart to enable each one to vote properly at a general election') that 'self-expression' becomes the expression of the self which, in fact, democracy wants to see, a self, moreover, which suffers from the insufficiencies which Lawrence has so acutely diagnosed and which have been analysed in the first section of this chapter.

For the dangers are infinite:

'A man who has not the soul, or the spirit, to learn and to *understand*, he whose whole petty education consists in the acquiring of a few tricks, will inevitably, in the end, come to regard all educated or understanding people as tricksters.'

Lawrence knew; he was of the people. He had learnt the lesson of his own father. After Mr. Lawrence had struggled through the first half-page of his son's first novel, the following conversation ensued:

' "And what did they gi'e thee for that, lad?"

[1] The notion behind *General Education in a Free Society*—the Harvard report, for instance. The writers tangle themselves up into the most delightful knots when the problem of what to give the less gifted arises—how to turn the weeds into rose-bushes. The curriculum for such people 'must not be simply watered-down versions of more complex courses but authentic and fresh vehicles of the spheres of general education—the world, man's social life, the realm of imagination and ideal—designed to implant the power of thought and expression, the sense of relevance and value'. How we love, in talking about education, to bemuse ourselves with words, delightful cosy abstractions, so comfortably remote from Lawrence's Jimmy Shepherd and the bottle factory (cf. *Education of the People*). The whole of this report deserves to be read with Lawrence in mind.

' "Fifty pounds, Father."

' "Fifty pounds!" He was dumbfounded, and looked at me with shrewd eyes, as if I were a swindler.

' "Fifty pounds! And tha's never done a day's work in thy life!" '

Perhaps to-day there is an even greater danger, now that education has gone down to meet 'the people', has become a matter of 'interest' and amusement, is conceived in terms of 'quizzes' and 'public forums'. It is the danger of the semi-literates' regarding their opinions as ultimate, the awful penalty of the false individuality we have so carefully nurtured, one of the tyrannies that this universalization of the 'idea' has introduced. As an expression of Lawrence's sense of what working-people have lost rather than gained through modern 'democratic' education, there is this quotation from one of his descriptions, reprinted in *Phoenix*: he is describing the coal-mining population of the Nottinghamshire countryside, the men he knew so well from his youth:

'The people lived almost entirely by instinct; men of my father's age could not really read. And the pit did not mechanize men. On the contrary. Under the butty system, the miners worked underground as a sort of intimate community, they knew each other practically naked, and with curious close intimacy, and the darkness and underground remoteness of the pit "stall", and the continual presence of danger, made the physical, instinctive and intuitional contact between men very highly developed, a contact almost as close as touch, very real and very powerful. This physical awareness and intimate *togetherness* was at its strongest down pit. When the men came up into the light they blinked. They had, in a measure, to change their flow. Nevertheless, they brought with them above ground the curious dark intimacy of the mine, the naked sort of contact and if I think of my childhood it is always as if there was a lustrous sort of inner darkness, like the gloss of coal, in which we moved and had our real being. My father loved the pit. He was hurt badly, more than once, but he would never stay away. He loved the contact, the intimacy, as men in the war loved the intense male comradeship of the dark days. They did not know what they lost till they lost it. And I think it is the same with the young colliers to-day. . . . The great fallacy is, to pity the man. He didn't dream of pitying himself, till agitators and sentimentalists taught him to. He was happy: or more than happy, he was fulfilled.'

A romantic picture?—possibly; there was the poverty and the men's lack of responsibility, like Mr. Morel's shiftlessness in *Sons and Lovers*. Yet, after all, Lawrence knew—it was part of his life. And his attitude deserves at least as much attention as that of the social worker; at least, Lawrence knew from the inside; he was *of* the culture and possessed therefore Mr. Eliot's 'imaginative understanding' of it.[1]

And so there is another danger lurking in 'self-expression', according to Lawrence; the danger of the false idea of self in the child and the encouragement that current practice gives it; the incapacity of the child to know truly what basically it wants. The child all too readily, as we have seen, becomes the victim of its own mind:

'It is part of our sentimental and trashy creed to-day that a little child is most purely himself, and that growing up perverts him away from himself. We assume he starts as a spontaneous little soul, limpid, purely self-expressive, and grows up to be a sad sophisticated machine. Which is all very well, and might easily be so, if the mind of the little innocent didn't start to work so soon, and to interfere with all his little spontaneity.'

He sees the soap and wants it, as Lawrence says; not because he really wants the soap but because he has got the incipient idea into his head that he wants the soap. Animals can sniff and pass on; but not human beings. They get the *idea* of what they want in their heads . . . and nearly poison themselves in the realization, as the child does with the soap. And so

'Instead of waiting for the wisdom out of the mouths of babes

[1] Cf. p. 46.

and sucklings, let us see that we keep the soap-tablet out of the same mouths.'

And that means that we have got to accept our responsibilities as educators and as adults. This idea of responsibility is Lawrence's great contribution to the controversy. The child cannot be responsible for himself. The need to keep the soap out of the child's mouth makes self-expression a dishonest farce; just as the necessity for 'kerb-drill', for instance, makes a farce of it in our schools to-day.[1] And so

'We've got to educate our children, and it's no light responsibility. We've got to try to educate them to that point where at last there will be a perfect correspondence between the spontaneous, yearning, impulsive-desirous soul and the automatic *mind* which runs on little wheels of ideas.'

'We've got to decide for our children', because they can't decide for themselves; and by doing so, if we do so 'seriously and reverently', we free them by helping them to come into their deep selves, by protecting them from 'Northcliffe and trade unions'. And yet, of course, as we have seen, we don't do it to-day. 'Freedom for youth' means, in the main, freedom to be corrupted by every meretricious influence that our civilization has spawned—and it has been more fertile than most—not the freedom to come to their soul's understanding.

Lawrence's notions of adult responsibility—the responsibilities of parents and teachers on which he so much insisted— follows the usual pattern of apparent contradictoriness. It is a mixture of a 'fine and delicate and fierce discipline' and a complete forgetfulness of the child's existence; not the anxious, hovering, conscious forgetfulness of the child psychology and

[1] I have never been able to understand why we hedge the bodies of our children with such rigid imposed restrictions—no self-expression in front of the motor car, no free play with the knife and fork at school dinners, not even a little playful micturation in the classroom—and yet, if some of our educational idealists were listened to, we should allow their eternal souls to be at the beck and call of any passing whim that happened to stir their little minds.

welfare victim, but a fine indifference and oblivion. It follows the rhythm of essential discipline and freedom; such a rhythm, however, is not, for the modern teacher and parent, easy to attain; it is only possible to people who possess their own souls.

Lawrence appreciates the basic conflict of wills that lies at the bottom of all human relationships and which modern democratic psychology tends to gloss over. He analyses this conflict as it affects school-relationships, in *The Rainbow*:

'So there existed a set of separate wills, each straining itself to the utmost to exert its own authority. Children will never naturally acquiesce to sitting in a class and submitting to knowledge. They must be compelled by a stronger, wiser will, against which will they must always strive to revolt. So that the first great effort of every teacher of a large class must be to bring the will of the children into accordance with his own will. And this he can only do by an abnegation of his personal self, and an application of a system of laws, for the purpose of achieving a certain calculable result, the imparting of certain knowledge. Whereas Ursula thought she was going to become the first wise teacher by making the whole business personal, and using no compulsion. She believed entirely in her own personality.

'So that she was in a very deep mess . . . she was offering to a class a relationship which only one or two of the children were sensitive enough to appreciate, so that the mass were left outsiders, therefore against her.'

Lawrence thus shows how the conception of *personal* relationship as applied to children, especially, needs to be mitigated. More about this will be said in the next chapter. For the moment it is sufficient to question whether modern education, which strives to harness the egotistical will of the child through rational persuasion and 'interest', is sufficiently aware of what it is about. These 'spiritual' 'mind' elements (as Lawrence would call them), in children at any rate, are too little developed and too weak to overcome the fundamental egotistic drives; nor perhaps, if one accepts Lawrence's views on the dangers of the stimulation of the 'upper centres' in children, is it advisable that such incentives should be so pervasively employed.

There is none of the modern sloppiness in the Lawrentian discipline, because there is none of the modern love idealism in it. Lawrence's discipline is based on the essential difference between adult and child. The emotional dangers of anything else, any introduction into the child world of a demand for adult responses, is, Lawrence considers, death to the possible development of the child:

'. . . parents should never try to establish adult relations, of sympathy or interest or anything else, between themselves and their children.'

To do so is to over-emphasize the spiritual centres of development, when there is no corresponding recompense possible in vital sex relationship; hence a starving of the supremely important lower centres. And so

'Parents should remain parents, children children for ever, and the great gulf preserved between the two. Honour thy father and thy mother should always be a leading commandment. But this can only take place when father and mother keep their true parental distances, dignity, reserve and limitation. As soon as father and mother try to become the *friends* and *companions* of their children, they break the root of life, they rupture the deepest dynamic circuit of living, they derange the whole flow of life for themselves and their children.'

There is no doubt that in all this, Lawrence is speaking from the depths of his personal experience. The bitter chapter on 'Parent Love' in the *Fantasia* is an indication of how well he had absorbed the lesson of his mother, and of what his relation with her had cost him in his subsequent relationships. Like the parent he there condemns, she had roused in him the 'dynamic response of (her) own love-will', a sort of 'dynamic *spiritual* incest, more dangerous than sensual incest, because it is more intangible and less instinctively repugnant'. His constant exhortations to parents to repulse the child, push it away, prevent its clingingness, must be understood in relation to his own experience. And, as has been pointed out, his experience is merely that of many thousands of young men, whose parents (and not infrequently teachers, after the manner of Ursula Brangwen,[1]) have satisfied their own emotional longings at the expense of the emotional development of their children; the only difference is that Lawrence was more conscious of what had happened. How often the bitterness spurts out:

'Would God a she-wolf had suckled me, and stood over me with her paps, and kicked me back into a rocky corner when she'd had enough of me. It might have made a man of me.'
And again: 'No wonder they say geniuses mostly have great mothers. They mostly have sad fates.'

And so this profound understanding of the significance of one of the vital points of his life, this *impersonal* realization of what his mother did for him, explains and validates Lawrence's views on adult responsibility . . . the two sides of 'leave them alone' and of the proud manly discipline. But always the adult *responsible,* not a mere rejection . . . which is why I have called it an *impersonal* realization a few lines above. For Lawrence didn't rest in negative rejection; he had a positive view of the relationship of adult and child, to replace the parasitic emotionalism he condemned out of his soul's experience. And this positive notion springs from his realization of the need of mutual integrity in difference:

'Leave him alone. He is not you and you are not he. He is never to be merged into you nor you into him. Though you love

---

[1] Ursula in *The Rainbow* provides a perfect example of an apparently disinterested 'love' which yet is purely self-regarding and serves only to fulfil an emotional longing in the teacher:

'She dreamed how she would make the little, ugly children love her. She would be so *personal.* Teachers were always so hard and impersonal. There was no vivid relationship. She would make everything personal and vivid, she would give herself, she would give, give, give all her great stores of wealth to her children, she would make them *so* happy, and they would prefer her to any teacher on the face of the earth.'
The last clause gives the clue.

him and he love you, this is but a communion in unfathomable difference, not an identification into oneness.'

And so it is not a question of neglect, but an integral part of his scheme to aid all to come to their fulfilment of themselves, in themselves and not through other people:

'A child must learn to contain itself. It must learn to sit still if need be. Part of the first phase of education is the learning to stay still and be physically self-contained.'

If the adult must not be parasitic on the child, so must the child learn not to impose on the adult: 'a child must learn not to bother another person.' But always responsibility:

'But always remember that it is a single little soul by itself; and that the responsibility for the wise, warm relations is yours, the adult's. . . . But never forget your own honour as an adult towards the small individual. It is a question of honour, not love.'

And again: 'It is the business of parents *mentally* to forget but dynamically never to forsake their children.'

From this emerge the other aspects of Lawrence's notions of child-adult relationship. What the child does, it must do well. Watch its deportment. Make it pay attention: 'The soul must give earnest attention, that is all.' And, of course, no 'self-expression'.

'Down with imagination in school, down with self-expression. Let us have a little severe hard work, good, clean, well-written exercises, well-pronounced words, well-set-down sums: and as far as head-work goes, no more. . . . Let us have a bit of solid, hard, tidy work. And for the rest, *leave the children alone.*'

And when they annoy, don't be afraid, in honest anger, to smack them; at least better that than the ideal bullying that goes on. . . . 'What would mummy say if . . .', 'Surely you love Daddy too much to. . . .' The smack hurts and is over; it springs from a vital 'blood' relationship; and it offers much less possibility for self-conscious posturings, opportunity for the child to offer an 'ideal' personality to fit his calculation of the situation:

'Quick, quick, mothers of England, spank your wistful babies. Good God, spank their little bottoms; with sharp, red anger spank them and make men of them. Drive them back. Drive them back from their yearning, loving parasitism; startle them for ever out of their angelic wistfulness; cure them with a quick wild yell of all their wonder-child spirituality. Sharp, sharp, before it is too late. . . . Let us get this wide, wistful look out of our children's eyes—this oh-so-spiritual look, varied by an oh-so-spiteful look.'

It is interesting to consider, for a moment, the serious decline of spanking among middle-class parents, especially those of some intellectual pretensions—I mean, of course, spanking in Lawrence's motivation of the term, not the indiscriminate slapping that merely indicates the parents' ill-nature and resentment. One can list quite a number of causes: the democratic humanitarian feeling that physical violence in any of its guises is to be deprecated; the preference for mutual 'understanding' leading to agreement—children now are to be given reasons for everything they do; garbled Freud, proving that any kind of repression is wrong; the absence of any real standards among the parents; the influence of American child conduct; sentimental ideas about childhood as an age of innocence; the fear of being accused of sadism; even more sentimental notions about the child knowing best; the extension of democratic egalitarianism and the abstract notion of 'rights' to children; the nerveless acquiescence before the vitality of 'youth'; sheer laziness; the absence of real, passionate behaviour. But one of the chief reasons, in the absence of any real religious emotional outlet in society, is the way in which parents have come to find some of their emotional fulfilment in their relationship with their children. I always remember a friend of mine who had a child of almost uncontrollable naughtiness and wilfulness explaining why he couldn't slap him: 'I couldn't bear that a child of mine should shrink from me.' It is easy to see the self-protectiveness in what at first sight seems to be an admirably humane statement.

After all, we exist in love and anger, so let us admit it; only let the love be proper to the occasion, a sending out of tenderness from an inviolable soul, not a yearning for a completion *out* of the other; and let the anger be a 'sharp, fierce reaction: sharp discipline, rigour; fierce, fierce severity' to rouse the child and bring him to his soul's pride:

'You *must* fight him, tooth and nail, if you're going to keep him healthy and alive. And if you're going to be able to love him with warm, rich bowels of love, my heaven, how you must fight him, how openly and fiercely and with no nonsense about it.'

And one must do this to children, not only to love them, but to make them free and proud: 'If a boy slouches out of a door, throw a book at him, like lightning'; don't stand for degenerate,

'nervous, twisting, wistful, pathetic centreless children we are cursed with: or the fat and self-satisfied, sheep-in-the-pasture children who are becoming more common: or the impudent, I'm-as-good-as-anybody smirking children who are far too numerous.'

Above all, remember 'Where there is no pain of effort there is a wretched, drossy degeneration'. For once more it must be emphasized, 'The plain fact is that parents and teachers *are* responsible for the bearing and developing of their children, so they may as well accept the responsibility flatly, and without dodges'. After all, 'The tyranny of Power is no worse than the tyranny of No-Power'. We do not solve the problem by transferring power to the children.

Finally, we need to consider one of the most revolutionary of Lawrence's suggestions, though one that emerges quite naturally from the views already expounded. He believed, as we have seen, in the radical inequality of mankind, an inequality which has both a positive and a negative side to it. When, therefore, he suggests that the masses are incapable of mind-consciousness, he is concerned to free them, not to enslave them; they are 'To give active obedience to their leaders, and to possess their own souls in natural pride'. It is the same ideal that lies behind Henry V's, the Elizabethan ideal king's, statement: 'Every subject's duty is the king's; but every subject's soul is his own.' The whole of Henry's speech, indeed, is worth reading as a counterblast to certain modern theories of responsibility. Obedience and freedom, in these terms, balance one against the other; for by handing over the responsibility which belongs to the leaders and which the masses are in any case incapable of exercising, they become free to exercise the responsibilities that lie within their grasp . . . the immediate *personal* responsibilities instead of the high abstract ones which they can't understand . . . 'the whole thing should work upwards, every man voting for that which he more or less understands, through contact'. The key appears in the last phrase—'through contact' —through blood understanding, not abstract mental understanding, of which the masses are, for the most part, incapable.

All this lies behind the categorical statement that appears in the *Fantasia*:

'*The great mass of humanity should never learn to read and write— never.*'

The elementary school, in any case, Lawrence considers, falls down between the false idealism of every weed a rose-bush and the 'profound cynicism of the laundry and the bottle-factory at the bottom of everything', in our vile industrialized community. Between the two, both the child *and the teacher* (public clown, Lawrence called him) are degraded:

'The elementary school-teacher is in a vile and false position. Set up as a representative of an authority which has absolutely no base except in the teacher's own isolate will, he is sneered at by the idealists above and jeered at by the materialists below.'

The situation, after all, is not so radically different from what it was in Lawrence's own day. Our latter-day idealists have set up the secondary modern school, the purpose of which no one really yet knows, for all the high-sounding Ministry platitudes. For Whitehall may use some of Lawrence's own phrases about fulfilment; but when these notions are not embedded in the rich concreteness of Lawrence's vision, when they are not sustained by that remarkable insight into our present ills that Lawrence had, they lose their point.[1]

They have become what Lawrence so vehemently condemned ... mental abstractions, as remote from the living experience of child and teacher as the abstractions of Mr. Gradgrind and his insistence on 'fact'. Our modern sickly pandering to the child-ego, every little Bill Smith as good as anyone else, all life a grand cosy little happy togetherness, at worst a sort of friendly competition, where everyone wins, as in Alice's Caucus-race, every child a certificate and no failures, is more corrupting than a little acquaintance with impersonal fact. So we see the virtues of Lawrence's curriculum: 'Abolish all the bunkum, go back to the three R's.' Hard work and, if necessary, big classes: 'The *personal* element, personal supervision is of no moment.' Something objective, clean and tidy, properly done with all the soul's attention. No more smatterings and pretty lispings, no creeping, underground flattery such as we suffer from at the moment. No more smirking 'encouragement' but an insistence on a job properly done. Teachers in possession of their own souls, and as a result children in possession of theirs. Children as children not little sophisticated, self-conscious Shirley Temples, flattering their parents' self-esteem ('For, oh, dear me! *what* a feather in the cap of a mortal mother is an infant prodigy.') And a respect once more for learning and vital knowledge as something requiring 'hard, hard work', like Lawrence writing *The Rainbow* eight times, not the prerogative of any one of the low on whom

---

[1] A fine example springs to hand in the week in which I write. An Inspector of Further Education is recommending the teaching of shorthand and typing and 'commercial' subjects: 'The aim (of education) was total education, the full development of the child's character and possibilities. This, where necessary, could be achieved through the teaching of commercial as well as general subjects, and therefore, in areas where commerce was of particular importance and where it would be to the child's advantage to have some knowledge of the subject, why should education not have a commercial bias?' (*The Times Educational Supplement*—summary.) The technique seems to be to take a high-sounding formula and then to persuade people that anything one wants to recommend forwards its professed intention.

assurance cares to sit. When you come to look at it, if you can look at it through the haze of educational experts—and God knows, they would cover the sun anywhere—it's not such an unattractive programme.

Yet, of course, I do not put Lawrence forward as providing a *programme*. Obviously, for instance, no government would close the schools, as Lawrence advocates. In any case, to do so would not solve the problem of self-consciousness. But I do advocate him as someone who asks the *real* questions, who saw modern society for what it is and who therefore saw the education, which is intended to bolster and proliferate the type of person this society spawns, in a novel and revealing light. In any case, he dares to probe where no other modern educationalist even ventures. Always, in Lawrence, one has that feeling of contact with a real personality; to read the *Fantasia* after so much of modern nerveless, conveyor-belt writing on education is to receive the vitalizing and invigorating effect of a mental cold bath; it cleanses at least. There is a sentence in *The Rainbow* which hits off Lawrence remarkably well: 'There was a bristling rousedness in the room.' There always is in any room that Lawrence enters; it's why we need to let him into the schoolroom a little.

Again, and it must be re-emphasized, it would be more than useless—as Lawrence himself makes clear—to *apply* his ideas as ideas; to do so would be to fall into the very error he himself condemned.[1] What Lawrence gives us is a series of vividly exploratory excursions into the central vastnesses of present human consciousness, where so few of the rest have ever ventured. What he brings back leads to an extension of awareness and being in our educational concerns. He does not provide a series of formulae to be applied mechanically; but neither is what he says to be ignored except as a polite study. At least he was one of those moderns—perhaps the only one—concerned with self

---

[1] Cf. Lawrence's rebuke to his wife when they were out horse-riding, and Mrs. Lawrence spoke of the vitality she received from the horse, 'Don't be silly, Frieda, you don't feel anything of the sort—you've simply been reading my books.' (I quote from memory.)

who, in the practice of his novels, transcended self to an amazing degree and achieved a richness and even a harmony. Thus what he has to say must inform and enrich the educator, serve as a living principle of understanding. If we come to see the current set-up in a new light—and I believe we must—we shall need the strong illumination, the *difference* of vision that Lawrence had. At least the educational psychologist needs to consider, deeply, what Lawrence has to reveal about the nature of human life.

Finally, he is not the whole story. Obviously what he has to offer is precarious and depends upon the peculiar honesty of a unique individual. He needs to be seen in his totality; for much the same sort of language, out of context, has been used by a Hitler.[1] There may be some truth—though I would not push this too far—in Mr. Eliot's remark that Lawrence is the first rather than the last word, that his value is cleansing and cathartic and that his sense of order is too precarious—or at least too liable to misunderstanding (no one, in fact, has been more perverted) to provide a safe guide. And yet, against this, he has the right fundamental conception of freedom, leading to order. 'There is nothing at all to be gained from disunion, disintegration and amorphousness. . . . There must be system'— but an organic, not a mechanical one; there must even be tradition. 'Alvina watching him, as if hypnotized, saw his old beauty, formed through civilization after civilization.' But what Lawrence only reaches towards in this way Newman and Eliot provide. They and Lawrence are complementary; and they meet on the third ground—the ground beyond personality. That ground, so far as it affects education, now needs a little more explicit exploration.

[1] It is surely hardly necessary to point out that the very depth of Lawrence's concern for people and their genuine spiritual health, his fundamental respect for human personality which yet saw it for what it is and still so devoutly cared, is sufficient to protect him from any naive accusations—that have in fact been made—of fascist tendencies.

CHAPTER SEVEN

AUTHORITY IN EDUCATION

'How could communities,
Degrees in schools, and brotherhoods in cities . . .
But by degree, stand in authentic place?
Take but degree away, untune that string,
And, hark! what discord follows.'
—SHAKESPEARE: *Troilus and Cressida*

It will be seen that in all three writers whose educational ideas I have expounded in the last three chapters there is inherent a conception of authority, an authority through which man achieves his freedom and dignity, and the acceptance of which is a pre-requisite to the attainment of such freedom. For Arnold, that authority is an humanistic one; a 'centre of enlightened opinion' is to preserve standards in our society, and of course, a state composed of our 'best' selves. But there is a certain egocentricity in Arnold, a hint of smugness and self-satisfaction, a lack of awareness that makes his conception, perhaps, a partial one. Both Newman and Lawrence appeal to an extra-human authority. Newman expresses his allegiance to a traditional 'form', a 'form' in which was inherent a recognition of the dignity of man as a creature of God, and the possibility of fulfilment of the sort that Newman himself attained; but his allegiance involved the free 'assent' of the personality, and his 'order' is thus dependent upon an initial act of the individual. Lawrence probes the inner recesses of man's being and finds his dignity and authority there; but to his exploration of the psychic depths he is initially led by something beyond personality which involves the creation of new 'forms' and a more delicate system; his individuality exists within a framework of 'order', a 'givenness' in human nature.

It seems to me that the most pressing problem of the moment in education—as in the whole of our social life—is the search for an 'authority' that will give strength and meaning to man's free development of himself that will allow man to come to his true 'self', in Lawrence's significance of the term—which, in the last resort, is what education implies. That authority cannot be found within the circle of the self, nor can it be found in terms of other selves only. I think the investigation into the current inadequacies of 'freedom' and 'order' in Chapters Two and Three showed that; and Arnold, despite his persistent finenesses, is something of a portent as well as a hope.

But I can allow Arnold, Newman and Lawrence to speak for themselves. In this chapter I am concerned with something narrower and, in a sense, more practical; though, at the same time, I would have it remembered that what I have to say has at the back of it ideas derived from my three 'authorities'. It is, in any case, perhaps time that I offered a few more particular judgements, and showed something of the relevance of what I have been saying to the classroom. What, then, is the significance, purpose and function of authority in education? In what sorts of ways will the acceptance of the notion of 'authority' affect our day to day handling of educational problems? I have made a number of criticisms of current practices; I have invoked an older tradition, though at the same time I have, I trust, made it clear that in doing so I look for no arbitrary imposition, no dead handling which will abrogate all the vital knowledge about the learning process, child development, etc., which has been so usefully gained during the last thirty or forty years. The new techniques—many of them at any rate—have a vital part to play, provided they are controlled by a keen and fastidious awareness of the purposes they are intended to subserve. But 'learning', I believe, matters; and the teacher as *agent*, as *representative* is important.

We need, first, to see the problem in a limited, historical setting. In doing so a certain repetition of ideas and conceptions from the previous chapters may be necessary; but it is important to see the specific problem of authority in its contemporary guise.

The problem of authority is one that is present in most social configurations; but it is one that has been consistently glossed over since the first world war put paid to so many of the traditional modes of social behaviour that had come down from the nineteenth century. To understand the current uncertainty about the nature of authority in the schools it is, I think, necessary to see that such indecision only reflects the doubt and confusion that exist in wider social spheres. The liberal humanitarian democratic tradition, which, despite state planning, is still strong in most cultivated circles to-day, based its notion of human nature on assumptions concerning the ultimate rationality of mankind; hence the widespread attempt to substitute rational argument, manifested as democratically agreed solutions, for the old authoritative direction in current power situations. Co-partnership in industry is an example that springs to mind . . . the attempt in the sphere of industrial relationships, to obviate the possible antagonism of the worker by giving him a voice in the complex business of management.

The widespread revolt against authority came after the first World War, partly as a reaction against the supposed bungling of the 'old men' and partly in general deprecation of 'public spiritedness' fostered by the intellectuals of the day. When Mr. Clive Bell—to quote a reasonably respectable source—proclaimed that civilized man desired 'complete self-development and complete self-expression' he spoke for a generation which developed the habit of turning to the self for enlightenment and recognized no other authority. The intellectuals of the twenties, indeed, exercised a great influence in the decline of the notion of authority in human affairs. They both manifested and furthered the depreciation of any standard outside the self; and in this doctrine of self, this emphasis on the private state of the mind, they were strengthened by having behind them a philosophy which had been formulated at Cambridge in the early years of the century. Under the influence of Moore's *Principia Ethica*, a group of brilliant young men set out a philosophy of life and conduct which in after years, when they had all moved to Bloomsbury, was to form a dominating motif in the nineteen-twenties. Maynard Keynes described the fundamentals of the faith, and his exposition has been published posthumously. His description so exactly defines the spirit informing the outlook of these writers that it is worth recalling:

'Nothing mattered except states of mind, our own and other people's, of course, but chiefly our own. These states of mind were not associated with action or with achievement or with consequences. They consisted in timeless, passionate states of communion, largely unattached to "before" or "after". Social action as an end in itself and not merely as a lugubrious duty . . . dropped out of our Ideal, and not only social action, but the life of action generally, power, politics, successes, wealth, ambition, with the economic motive and the economic criterion.'

How well this fitted in with a generation that had seen all too much of power and politics and social action. A few of the progenitors may have grown somewhat beyond the theory—but by no means all. And so what had originally been directed against the Fabian spirit and Utilitarianism became part of the mental protest of a whole generation. The emphasis on immediate feeling, pure experience as the only realities, obviated the search for agreed objective moral values. Values based on anything but the beholder's purely personal state of mind are essentially the products of continuity and tradition; and continuity and tradition had been finally broken. The danger always is that values once generally accepted will harden into conventions; and conventions, according to Mr. Clive Bell, were 'limitations on thought, feeling and action' and 'the enemies of originality and character, hateful, therefore, to men richly endowed with either'. Hence the aptness of a philosophy which, to return once more to Keynes, 'recognized no moral obligation . . . no inner sanction to conform or to obey'. Perhaps it is hardly necessary to be assured that with this went 'supreme self-confidence, superiority and contempt towards the rest of the unconverted world'. Arnold's Philistine was still the bogy; 'the life of a first-rate English man or woman' urged Mr. Bell 'is one long assertion of his or her personality in the face of unsympathetic or actively hostile circumstances.' Now, rebelliousness always involves the assertion of the ego; at the same time it usually has an object beyond mere assertion. When external purpose is lacking what might be termed total rebellion can become as childish as total acceptance. The danger was not always avoided. At the same time, despite the distaste for the Philistine, there was breathed abroad a large spirit of tolerance: 'There must be no taboos, no closed subject', asserted Mr. Bell. Everything in fact was to be tolerated, except intolerance; for intolerance was often the product of a sense of sin, and a sense of sin, he shuddered, was 'nothing more than a remnant of barbarism, which would yield to treatment'. Such superstitions, indeed, robbed life of 'half its glory and a good part of its fun'. The intellect was to be free to handle what it chose, not only in earnest but in fun too—in fact, chiefly in fun. Did not Virginia Woolf take to task Logan Pearsall Smith when he objected to intellectual writers making contributions to fashionable magazines, and, as he put it, 'preaching to the butterflies'; so that between 'articles on Cosmetics, and advertisements of Exclusive Underwear' there were to be found 'little snippets of butterfly-dishes of Art and Culture'. It was people like him, she said, 'respectabilities and solemnities and humbugs, who were the enemies of unfettered thought in England'; such people 'deliberately did their best to stifle all freedom, all rebellion, all ribaldry, in the English press'.

The unfettered and rebellious mind, then, seeking ecstasies of experience and unfettered by traditional moral scruples, was the version of the good life offered by the fashionable intellectuals in the twenties, when 'progressive' education first became the conventionally accepted mode for the aspiring 'intellectual' classes. Mr. Eliot's movement towards 'tradition' and 'orthodoxy' had not yet gathered weight. Mr. E. M. Forster expressed his preference for his friend over his country and thus revealed the only claim over the self that most people were prepared to admit . . . the claim implicit in the idea of personal relationships. But even here there existed no objective standard in terms of which personal relationships might take on significance. Lawrence provides the appropriate comment, which I have already quoted:

'Is there nothing beyond my fellow man? If not, then there is nothing beyond myself, . . . my neighbour is but myself in a mirror. So we toil in a circle of pure egoism.'

When personality becomes an end in itself or exists only in terms of other 'personalities', it suffers an inevitable diminution of the sort implicit in Lawrence's comment; relationship serves only itself instead of attaining an enrichment by seeking a purpose which exists beyond the pure togetherness, as would happen in a truly religious community, when human intercourse was guided by standards beyond the felt need of the moment.

Now there have been other forces at work which have helped to destroy the notion of authority in human affairs but these two, the rationalist assumption and the incapacity to see beyond the personal, will do. For the moment, what I have to say will be confined to the latter; I will comment on the inevitable restriction in our educational undertakings which has resulted from the current demand that children should understand the *nature* of what they are studying a little later.

It is, then, about the 'personal' element in education that I wish to raise a preliminary query. Observation would show that deep personal relationships are only possible between minds that carry a certain weight of common assumption. The offer needs to be met by a reciprocation for a genuine fruitful relationship to spring up. And such common ground provides something which exists beyond the immediate exigencies of relationship in terms of which the relation can take on significance.

This is one of the key points, it seems to me, where our efforts to extend notions based upon reciprocated personal intercourse, of the sort I have been speaking of above, to teacher—child relationships must inevitably fail. The desire to mitigate the harshness of Victorian 'discipline' in schools, in many respects very praiseworthy, has nevertheless led us to forget certain inevitable and unavoidable features of the classroom situation. The school necessarily involves an authoritative set-up. The Teacher, however much he may attempt to disguise the fact, must, if only because he is not appointed or dismissed by the pupils, represent an authority. He must do so, also, because he is inescapably 'other' than the children. For one thing, he is older; he has inevitably undergone experiences which give him a different background of assumption from that of his charges. He is, that is to say, psychically different. He has, too, certain legal responsibilities and is answerable to the community at large for aspects of his behaviour. There is therefore unavoidably, 'mechanically', as it were, a gulf which no attempt at disguise can hide, because it is endemic in the situation, 'given'. Nor do I think that it should be disguised. Power is an inescapable element in adult life, to which we all at some time or other have to come to terms; and I deprecate a great deal of the current insincerity which strives to hide the true situation and thus prepares the child for a fictitious world, not one of reality, even when the circumstance is blanketed under some such grandiose title as 'training in the self-responsibilities of citizenship'. It is to be deprecated for a number of reasons, not least of which is the need to learn respect for the idea of authority as such, as a necessary element in the proper functioning of the community.

Against this it may well be urged that the self-responsibility that a democratic community requires would be more forwarded by enabling more children to have the opportunity of 'learning by their mistakes' (the usual excuse given by educationalists); it seems to me that the full implications of this procedure have not been sufficiently realized. For in what sort of way is the pupil to appreciate even the possibility of making a mistake unless he makes a prior submission, partly to the matter of his study and partly to the superior wisdom and taste of his mentor who derives his 'authority' from the discipline in which he is instructing? The ability to respond more deeply can, in any learning situation, only go along with a submission to the superior capacity of the teacher to demonstrate subtleties beyond the untrained receptivities of the pupil to understand. In other words, the fact of authority, however subtly disguised, enters into the pursuit of all knowledge. Learning always involves a determination to grasp after what is as yet uncomprehended. It requires, on the part of the learner, a respect for the unknown, a reverence before the unattained; inevitably, therefore, a transcendance of self. All learning presupposes an act of faith, a faith that there is, in fact, something to be learnt. There is a necessary sense in which values have to be recreated each time by each individual; but any such recreation is paradoxically dependent upon a previous acknowledgement of their existence.

So, unless the respect for authority, the authority of the subject, the authority of the teacher (which derives from the subject), exists, learning becomes impossible. The modern idea that the acceptance of or respect for value goes no further than the individual's capacity for rational comprehension would only be possible in an era which makes man the measure of all things and his personal standard the only criterion. One at least of the advantages of living in a religious age was that the ultimate standard became what was by definition the Incomprehensible. The fact that to some people the results of artistic creation, for instance, will for ever remain a mystery does not in any way destroy the validity of that creation.

And so, in the pupil, the act of acceptance or the authority of the as yet unknown is an essential pre-requisite to learning; and where adults are concerned, we may well imagine that there is a possible conscious submission based on adult responsibility. But where children are involved, no such prior acceptance can be assumed. For the adult's rationally conscious willingness to accept the authority of that which is not comprehended needs to be based on that which is comprehended; that of which I have no prior experience whatsoever does not exist for me even in a state of uncomprehension. Thus an adult's willingness to look further at pictures, to seek a deeper understanding of the processes of art can only be based on a prior experience (however slight) of looking at pictures. But experience in such matters does not come by the light of nature. Hence the need, where children are concerned, of a much fuller exercise of authority. For by the light of nature a child knows neither what he wants to do nor—as important—does he know what he doesn't want to do. For instance the playing of a musical instrument is a highly artificial occupation. Its delights only become apparent after a long and arduous apprenticeship. Such delights cannot possibly be apparent to a child, who sees before him only a series of exercises which it would be unfair to assume would 'interest' any child. Hence the need to impose the experience of practising the piano for at least a reasonable time so that the child shall be afforded an opportunity of deciding whether it wishes to pursue the study. As D. H. Lawrence says, we constantly need to make decisions for our children.[1]

Where many modern educationalists go wrong is in their failure to appreciate certain ambiguities in the idea of 'method'. There is so much current emphasis on methods and techniques of teaching that educationalists fail to recognize the necessary distinction between the technique and the end the technique is intended to serve. For instance, they seem to think that it is the method that provides the freedom; and that because they can speak of 'projects', 'free activities' and the like, they are ensuring the freedom of the child; for in such methods, they argue, authoritative guidance is reduced to a minimum, and therefore the child is 'free'.

Here they fall into the error of those who believe that freedom is the prerogative of a method and not the product of the accomplishment of an end. For all but the most temporary of

[1] I once had to study *Silas Marner* with a particularly backward school certificate form. It was not a book I would have chosen for these particular boys, but the alternatives were even less suitable. We studied the book with the closeness that the school certificate examination demands; and when I thought they must be heartily tired of it, I asked them if they would like to turn to some other work as a respite. No, one boy said, he would like to continue with *Silas Marner*. He hadn't liked it at first; but the necessity of close study had shown him things in the book which he would never have appreciated otherwise and which had made him change his mind. And the rest of the class concurred. Nor is this an isolated example.

human freedoms is dependent upon the discipline that has produced it, as should have been made clear in Chapter Three. Nothing could be more obviously untrue than the statement that man is born free.

Now, a concentration upon the idea of 'method', as the word is commonly interpreted, tends to hide the truth of this. For the common use of the word conceals the essential disciplinary function which a fuller consideration of 'method' reveals. There is, in fact, inherent in every field of learning, a specific 'method' of study which imposes itself, regardless of the idiosyncrasies of the learner. This method requires as of necessity the comprehension of a series of logical relationships, the omission of any one of which may well inhibit further progress—a fact which can be seen most clearly in mathematics, but which is a feature to a greater or lesser extent of all 'disciplines'. Thus, in this meaning of the word, to speak of 'free methods' is to perpetrate a contradiction in terms.

But this meaning of the term is all too frequently lost sight of. Instead, the word comes to refer to aspects of pupil-teacher relationship and to certain irrelevances which the teacher consciously introduces into the teaching of 'subjects' in order to make the matter more palatable to immature minds. It is to this sense of the word that for instance, Mr. Ford refers, in the article mentioned in Chapter Two, to a further consideration of which I will now turn, when he states that 'a conscientious teacher concerns himself endlessly about his teaching-methods, not in order to avoid encouraging a point of view, but so that his encouragement shall not be dogmatic or authoritarian'. But indeed, a teacher's encouragement can, in many spheres, be nothing but 'dogmatic and authoritarian'. Even in the province of values, there is a reasonably well defined hierarchy of taste which tradition, for those who care to seek it, has handed down and the reason for which, for those who are perpetually concerned to demand reasons, is usually susceptible to concrete demonstration and analysis. But in other subjects the dogmatism is inherent in their development, is an essential part of that 'authority' of the subject to which reference has been made above, and to which the teacher merely becomes the transmitting medium. Yet, of course, as a transmitting medium, the teacher need do no harm by adopting 'methods'—in the sense referred to in *this* paragraph—which introduce certain extraneous considerations (extraneous, that is, to the proper development of the subject in hand), in the hope of making the matter more easily assimilable, *provided always the fact that such considerations are extraneous is never lost sight of*. An easy example is provided by the introduction of social purpose into the teaching of arithmetic. The validity of the arithmetical processes of addition is quite independent of whether bills, marbles or what have you are being totted up. But adding up the household accounts is a quite legitimate 'method' of affording immediate relevance to processes which otherwise might be deemed too abstract for the child.[1]

But my italicized caveat in the last paragraph is one that is all too readily forgotten by those whose concern is for 'method' in Mr. Ford's use of the word. Thus the social purpose of adding up bills becomes the aim of learning arithmetic, which is to substitute the social purpose of tackling the household accounts as the real end of the learning of arithmetic instead of the learning of arithmetic itself. This inevitably involves certain restrictions on the pursuit of that subject and the further purposes, which may or may not be immediately social, which such pursuit would allow for. The fact that with some children the attainment of such a limited end is all that can be expected of their mental capacities is not reason for imposing such a limited aim on the rest.[2] And though I would not necessarily disapprove of such a limited aim for such children (together with other

[1] Though at the same time, it is worth noting that, whatever may have been the *origin* of arithmetical processes (whether social in the manner suggested by Hogben: *Mathematics for the Million* or not), the knowledge of the arithmetical process is now necessarily antecedent to its application. Thus the child can only calculate that three bars of chocolate at threepence a bar cost ninepence after he knows that three lots of three make nine. In other words the notion of number imposes itself upon this particular aspect of the social situation of chocolate buying.

[2] There is, sometime, an essay to be written, correlating the shift in the balance of political power with the changed emphasis in educational prac-

such activities extraneous to the study of arithmetic as the building of toy shops), I would emphasize the necessity of always being quite clear what it is we are about. But my observation of modern educational practice makes me think that we are not always by any means clear as to what we are about, that all too frequently we are placing far too much emphasis on the means and tending to substitute the possible end inherent in the means for the original end which the means were intended to subserve. And this leads to our mistaking a temporary and purely local freedom inherent in the means for a real and lasting freedom that can only emerge as the successful accomplishment of the original end. For though a child may indeed become free to shop, he is not free in the realm of those higher mathematical processes that are lost sight of in the accomplishment of the immediate social purpose, which should be a by-product only, though a useful one, to the learning of mathematics.[1]

That we are not always clear about the implications of our engagements is clear, I think, from a consideration of Mr. Ford's means for overcoming drudgery, of which he 'throws out a hint' in the same article. He begins by deprecating the idea that 'Facts like multiplication tables and simple arithmetic' (among others) are things that 'simply have to be learnt by heart'; it is such an attitude, he suspects, which produces children who 'just can't do maths.', etc. Mr. Ford then proceeds to indicate how such a regrettable state of affairs can be avoided. If, 'suitably presented of course', 'each subject is treated as a system of a particular kind, subserving certain ends and bearing distinct relations to material reality, many children find their feet far more quickly'.

tice. For it seems to me that an increasing concern for the needs of specific children—the less gifted, those whose capacities are limited narrowly to the 'social'—has led to many of our present attitudes.

[1] An extreme example of this confusion, leading to a perversion of ends, is provided in an account of a training college, published a short time ago. As *a feature of their English course*, the students erected a model post office. (*The Times Educational Supplement*, 21st February 1948, p. ·108.) What possible benefit to the study of English would derive from such a side-tracking of time and effort I find it difficult to comprehend.

Now I do not feel at all happy about the terms in which this is set out. For indeed, what ends that a child is capable of assimilating can some of the subjects with which Mr. Ford deals (arithmetic, history and languages) be said to subserve? That the subjects in question should be explicable to anyone in the terms which Mr. Ford suggests is highly doubtful. I take it that the ends which Mr. Ford regards the subjects as subserving are social ones. That, from his individual remarks on specific subjects, and from the knowledge one has of Mr. Ford's position, derived from the rest of his article, would seem a fair inference. Now, while I have no objection to temporary expedients, of the type indicated, being used as a means to further progress, to make as a precondition to that further progress an understanding of such social ends seems to me an example of putting the cart before the horse, of mistaken emphasis. It provides a further example of expenditure of energy on irrelevancies, leading to a possible undesirable delimitation of the syllabus. For Mr. Ford continues: 'They (the children) develop a confidence about the subject in proportion as they understand the kind of thing it is; and this can provoke sufficient excitement and wonder to help them take the drudgery in their stride.' This modern habit—an offshoot, I suspect, of nineteenth-century utilitarian rationalism—of requiring the child to comprehend the 'nature' of what he is doing, to appreciate the 'reasons' for pursuing one course of study rather than another, makes the child's experience of possible social situations the limiting factor in educational advance; for such 'reasons', to be comprehensible, can only be based on a very limited range of possible social repercussions, limited, that is to say, to the range of the child's social experience. In any case, such understanding of any pursuit of any real complexity is almost always impossible. How is it possible, for instance, to *explain* to the normal urban-bred grammar school child, with the culturally impoverished background that so many of them possess, the importance of the study of Greek, or even of their own language, to any degree of subtlety? The 'nature' of the thing to immature minds, only comes to be revealed in the course of the experience of it; and all too frequently, without the intervention of authority, the necessary grappling never takes place, or there is a pandering to the titillations of 'interest' which obviates any real coming to grips. It is the relative emphasis that is disquieting in Mr. Ford's diagnosis. There are introduced two categories: 'the kind of thing' a subject is—by which I take Mr. Ford to mean possible correlations with social experience—and the subject itself. And it would appear that the former is to take priority, as 'confidence about the new subject' (whatever that may mean) is dependent upon it. No piece of knowledge, however, is completely explicable in the terms of anything else; and Mr. Ford's conception of the process of learning, because of the mistaken stress mentioned above, seems to me pedagogically unsound. Nor need Mr. Ford regard my objections as hair-splitting; for when, in concrete educational situations, the building of post offices becomes part of the English course, there is obviously some very serious confusion of thought at work. And whereas Mr. Ford might well agree with me in condemning such activities as part of the English syllabus, he seems insufficiently aware that the course of education he favours gives an impetus to just such perverted undertakings.

Again, Mr. Ford seems to be unduly optimistic if he thinks that understanding, in his terms, necessarily provokes wonder and excitement sufficient to overcome drudgery. (He introduces, I know, the saving words 'help them to' before 'overcome'; but the terms of his assertion invite a strong repository of faith in the efficacy of such understanding.) The theory of the unconscious assimilation of unpalatable facts through temporary excitements of the play variety—'play' providing a social situation within which the working of the subject can be 'understood'—is one that in the experience of many teachers with whom I have discussed the subject is not borne out by the results. For teachers are becoming increasingly sceptical that by investing the subject with an immediate social significance of this sort (on which the success of the 'free method' largely depends) one necessarily provokes anything more than a temporary interest which in far too many children tends to peter out as soon as difficulties are encountered. So that even where the learning of tables is concerned, teachers need continually to impose their wills in the matter; and even after the results of play have been assimilated, there may still be necessary the mediaeval barbarities of drill! (And whereas the gain in social intercourse that results from 'play' methods may to some minds compensate for the lack of mathematical accuracy, it is as well to know what are likely to be the consequences of our new habits, and of the restrictive character of the standards we are adopting.)[1]

Mr. Ford's specific prescriptions for individual subjects go to confirm what has been written above, as well as to provoke strong dissent on their own account. A child—we are dealing with the beginners, be it remembered, those who are bothered with 'Facts like the multiplication tables and simple arithmetic, irregular verbs and the dates of history'—is to be 'shown that numerical relations are not a factual law of the universe but an intellectual convention, that the 'facts of history' are only a selection made and interpreted according to a given system of beliefs and from a given standpoint, and that irregular verbs are a fact only to the extent that they are seen as a product of social and cultural processes'. It is hard to believe that Mr. Ford is serious, or that I have understood him correctly. For even his saving clause, 'suitably expressed, of course', will not hide the absurdity of his pretensions. I can think, in my years of sixth-form teaching, of very few boys who might grasp such neo-Marxist conceptions, even suitably expressed. For indeed, to give only one example, I fail to see how anyone could appreciate

---

[1] Here are two recent comments: One is by a correspondent of *The New Statesman* (4th September 1948): 'American academic standards are lower than in our own schools . . . American schools . . . have been more adventurous than English State schools in trying out new methods. They are also more democratic, and they have paid the price of experimentation and democracy in lower standards of attainment.' The other comes from *English in Schools*, from an article by Miss Marion Hope Parker: '. . . . the result of the unfolding bud psychology has been to turn the primary school largely into an organization for developing cheerful social instincts. Its product usually has a healthy body but it is not safe to *assume* any further qualification other than a lack of self-consciousness. . . .'

the idea that the 'facts of history' are only a selection made and interpreted, etc.—in so far as they are—who has not already acquired a considerable number of such facts. Mr. Ford's ideas might well be dismissed, though unfortunately they seem to me the sort that are likely to bring educational theory into disrepute, were it not that the 'irrelevancies' of Mr. Ford's considerations—irrelevant, that is to say, to the pedagogical purposes Mr. Ford has in mind—provide a rough insight into the nature of certain epistemological errors which are adversely affecting modern educational theory. For what meaning of the word 'fact' could Mr. Ford produce that would deny a French verb a reality within a specific linguistic framework known as the French language? Yet he assures us that 'irregular verbs are a fact *only* to the extent that they are seen as a product of social and cultural processes' (never mind what relevance information about such processes would have to a child who was seeking to express himself in a foreign tongue for the first time).

But the dangerous results of Mr. Ford's attempt to deny significance to the various facts within their particular and specific frameworks is seen in the next paragraph. Mr. Ford considers it a waste that teachers should be left to develop their own subjects, 'because the full potentialities of their subjects are far more easily realized where the education of the school is treated as a developing whole, divisible only for the sake of convenience into distinct ends or distinct subjects or distinct themes'. Now Mr. Ford's declaration that it is only for the sake of *convenience* that the work of a school is divisible into distinct subjects merits attention. For one thing, it is an idea that, under various guises of expression, is bandied about a good deal. The project system, for instance, represents a distinct attempt to break down the so-called 'artificial barriers' between the subjects, by showing their interconnections based on a central theme, or centre of interest. Another frequent criticism of the study of separate subjects is that it leads to over-specialization. And so on.

Mr. Ford's assertion suggests that such division into 'subjects' is not obligatory, is not something imposed by the nature and authority of the subjects, but serves some much less vital purpose which he sums up under the term 'convenience'. Consideration, however, seems to me to show that such a belief cannot be seriously maintained. For though various subjects may be interrelated in certain ways, and the influence of events in one field of activity may have repercussions in other fields, in no way can such repercussions interfere with the significance of the 'event' within its own discipline and its essential correlations with other 'events' within the same field of study. Thus the knowledge that the wars of the seventeenth-century stimulated the desire for the solution of certain problems of ballistics and thus influenced, in ways which would need careful definition in specific instances, the nature of the investigation into the physical sciences, in no way affects the validity and 'reality' of such discoveries as were made, which are subject to the rules of verification proper to their own field, and which, once accepted as verified, take their place within a specific scientific framework. Thus in no way could it be said that the study of the history of the seventeenth century and the study of certain problems in ballistics are divided 'only for the sake of convenience'. The division is one that is imposed by the natures of the two 'subjects' and the correlations necessary within their own particular spheres of validity; though I would not deny that such scientific problems as we have been considering have, *considered as historical phenomena*, as problems, that is to say, which achieved solution at a specific time, their relevance to the study of seventeenth-century history, and thus belong to the field of historical relations as well.

A source of some uneasiness at the moment is the rather too glib way in which a number of teachers are embracing a bastard subject, usually known as 'Social Studies', in an attempt to give a coherence to their work which they think the normal subject divisions lack. This involves the introduction of some topic, usually of a social nature, within the scope of the child's immediate experience (such as, for instance, 'The town in which we live'), and using this as an agency for investigation into the various fields of study that relate themselves to this topic. Thus the history of the town will be studied, its geographical situation, its economic life, its social services, etc. In fact, it is a project of a particular kind. Now such study can be valuable provided teachers remember two things.

The significance of the specific information within each field of study (history, geography, etc.) will take its meaning to a considerable extent from its relation to other facts within the same field. Thus we sometimes hear it said that 'our town' gained its specific historical importance from, say, its geographical position on a river. But such historical importance is by no means explicable solely in terms of geographical position. There will be also a chain of historical occurrences which will have led to the foundation of a town on just that spot at that time. Thus the answer to the question 'Why did "our town" become a market town in the fourteenth century?' is not 'Because it stood on a river', though such a position may have been a contributing factor, but because a series of events have occurred within the field properly to be termed historical processes which have led to its foundation at just that time. An understanding of such events and therefore an understanding of why 'our town' came to be a market town at just such a time is therefore only possible in the light of information which a child cannot hope to have unless the subject division of 'history' is maintained. The necessity of subject teaching is thus not destroyed by the introduction of such projects, as some teachers seem to imagine; the authority of the subject, in fact, must be maintained.

Secondly, the study of specific topics like 'our town' inevitably implies a narrowing of the possible range of human experience available to the child. Now going from the known to the unknown—which the modern educationalist makes the basis of this type of instruction—has much to be said in its favour, provided the child realizes the contingency of the as yet unknown. This can only derive from his acceptance of the 'authority' of the subject; for the topic of the project quickly exhausts itself in a way in which the subject does not.

Thus such project studies are by no means to be avoided. But they are to be treated with considerable care for their limitations. They do not provide a satisfactory solution to the problem of the content of education. They are, of course, largely the result of the modern habit of regarding all human situations as the consequences of 'social processes'.

What Mr. Ford means when he goes on to speak of the education of the school being treated 'as a developing whole' I am not quite sure; I suspect that it is one of those deceptively ambiguous phrases which sound good and do away with the effort of clear thinking. Mr. Ford continues: 'This approach (i.e. the 'developing whole' business) is often the natural outcome of a system which keeps the child in the centre of the picture. Because each child is an entity, the education which is built around the child is most often a unified affair as well.' What does Mr. Ford imply by keeping 'the child in the centre of the picture'? In any *educational* situation (the 'picture', I take it, to which Mr. Ford refers) there are necessarily two elements—the child, and the knowledge the child is to acquire—as well as the teacher. To regard the child as the centre instead of as one of the two elements that have to combine, is to lay oneself open to just those errors I have examined in Chapter Three. The second sentence quoted above invites one or two preliminary questions. What is the function of the phrase 'most often'? Are we to understand that it is possible to build around a child (who is by definition always an entity) an education which is not a 'unified affair'? In which case, what will be the disintegrating factor in such a construction? It obviously can't be the child. But more important it is to ask what, in the cases where the education is duly unified, is to provide the unifying element? For 'is built around' suggests the necessity of a builder. Does he impose the unity on the structure? If he does, then his unification will be subject to those imperfections which are inevitable in human constructions and will be open to destruction, disintegration, as it were, at the hands of others. If it is the child, as an entity, that is to provide the unifying principle, how can such an entity within one class of substances impose a unity on something which belongs to quite a different order of substances? It may be that Mr. Ford, in making the child the centre of the picture,

means us to understand that he refers to those educational processes which are relevant to the immediate needs and interests
of the child; in which case these needs and interests impose a
temporary and quite artificial coherence ('artificial', that is to
say, to the nature of the various bodies of knowledge) within the
various disciplines on which the child's needs and interests im-
pinge. And if 'unification' in these terms is what Mr. Ford
means, he will find himself affording approval to an extreme
form of subjectivism which destroys any idea of a 'system',
which is open to all the objections to which such extreme subjectivism is commonly open (some of which emerge by implication in Chapter Three) and which makes nonsense of his
previous testimony to his 'profound belief' that 'taste is not
relative'.

The problem of authority in education, then, seems an inescapable one; and yet it is one that to my mind is not being
adequately tackled. What I have here aimed to accomplish has
been a twofold task; I have sought to reveal the ambiguities and
confusions inherent in many of the widely held educational
assumptions of the day; and I have sought to set out some of the
considerations that any profounder philosophy of education
would need to take into account, and which, it seems to me,
modern educationalists either forget or ignore. In the teacher
there is at once a human and an inhuman element; he is at once
an individual *and an agent*. For, he is not only himself but a
representative of the human heritage and the human tradition.
I do not wish to be misunderstood. It has always been part of
the glory of the English tradition that the school should be a
community; and the disposition of its parts and the relationships that form its being must take cognizance of that fact. In
any case, my comments on Arnold and Newman should make
it clear that I do not omit the 'human' factor; and in Newman's
case, at least, a deep regard for intellectual training was accompanied by a genuine concern for individuals. But a school is a
community with an object; it exists to serve a purpose beyond
the mere fortuitous social conglomeration of its individual elements. And if I have indicated that purpose aright then the

authoritative adjustments inside that community must be made with the proper object in mind. The teacher is not a Big Friend, diffusing 'smiles and soap' to his little band; he is the representative of something of vital importance beyond himself and he must make demands accordingly. And it must always be remembered that that 'something' is essential in the process of bringing man to a fullness of understanding of himself; it is no peripheral employment, the plaything of an arid academicism; it contains within itself the possibility of man's essential development and freedom, as Newman so clearly shows.

I am indeed alarmed lest too great a concentration on investigation into 'methods' should blind educationalists to the fact that there is taking place, subtly but none the less surely, a decided shift in the focus of educational attention; and that this shift manifests itself in an increasing inability to conceive valid ends to education. The exhilaration of new-found 'methods' seems to me to be contributing to the concealment of a very real restriction of scope and of a dangerous tendency to confuse means with ends, a state of affairs which is likely to lead, which indeed in the opinion of many teachers with whom I have discussed the matter, already has led, to a very definite decline in the quality of educational accomplishment in the country. By drawing attention to such a state of affairs, by asserting the objectivity of, and the authority inherent in, the various aspects of human knowledge, I hope to contribute positively to a more fundamental effort to tackle the whole nature of educational undertakings as they affect the day-to-day routine of our schools and colleges; so that while what is good in the new shall not be lost sight of, the essential need to conceive adequate ends within the tradition I have noted, the tradition of Newman and Eliot, leavened by the profound insight and understanding of Lawrence, shall be clearly recognized.

Not all, indeed, can profit equally from the tradition; but higher and lower natures can come equally to a fulfilment, can attain a valid resting-place in terms of an acceptance of that *other*, outside self, which the acceptance of an authoritative hierarchy in learning and comprehension permits; so that both 'higher' and 'lower' natures shall be 'free' within the framework of their understanding.

Part, indeed, of what is necessary is a realization of the *impersonal* element in education which Arnold, Lawrence and Newman, from their differing standpoints, stress. We need to recapture a sense of purpose, a common object which will at once inform and transcend the otherwise fortuitous relationship of master and pupil. As in our social life, so in our educational enterprises we need to meet on 'the third ground, the holy ground'; holy, at least, in the sense that human learning at once transcends the individual and social life, and that, informing its true spirit and its true essence there is the ultimate apprehension of the divine in man. For, paradoxically—and this is really the point—only thus are our 'freedom' and our 'individuality' safe. There is a greater human dignity involved in a *rightful* submission than in all the egocentric assertion of self which our superficial age so encourages. Something of what is involved in the notion of 'rightful' has, I hope, emerged both implicitly and explicitly in this book.

Man's 'spontaneous' individuality must not be sacrificed; rightly conceived, it is too precious a product of the modern world. But that 'spontaneity' and 'individuality', paradoxically, only comes to fruition in contact with high external purpose— or at least, in Lawrence's phrase, in doing things 'with the soul's attention'. This, at all levels, I consider essential. Where all minds are concerned, their individuality is best served by a grappling with, and a submission to, those higher 'objects' which human skill and learning invoke. 'To forget one's self, to surrender all personal feeling in the science of one's fine art, is the only way for a seaman to the faithful discharge of his trust' is the way the craft of the sea presented itself to Conrad in *The Mirror of the Sea* (a book which has its relevance in our diagnosis). Only in some such terms can our culture regain that quality which is so sadly lacking to-day— the quality which Arnold represents and reinforces.

INDEX

The main references are in bold type.